JAN 0 6 2016

DI062782

East Meadow Public Library
1886 Front Street, East Meadow, NY 11554
(516) 794-2570
www.eastmeadow.info

Growing Global:

Lessons for the New Enterprise

Growing Global:

Lessons for the New Enterprise

The Center for
Global Enterprise

A *Re-Think* series publication

Growing Global
© 2015 CGE. All rights reserved.

No part of this book may be reproduced in any form or by any means, electronic, mechanical, digital, photocopying or recording, except for the inclusion in a review, without permission in writing from the publisher.

Published in the USA by:
The Center for Global Enterprise
200 Park Avenue
Suite 1700
New York, NY 10166
http://thecge.net

Printed in the United States of America

ISBN: 978-0-9968580-0-7 (Hardcover)
         978-0-9968580-1-4 (Ebook)

Book design by Darlene Swanson • www.van-garde.com
Cover design by Daniel Swanson • www.van-garde.com

Table of Contents

Did You See It?

Samuel J. Palmisano

The world has changed — really changed — in the last ten years. And I suspect the pace of change is going to accelerate.

In 2005, I was two years into my tenure as CEO of IBM and I could see big changes unfolding in the business climate of the United States and of countries throughout the world. Global integration had transformed the corporate model and the nature of work itself. Ongoing technology advances were making it ever easier to trade, interact, and transact across geographic boundaries, time zones and languages. We saw that the new leaders would win not by surviving the storm, but rather by fundamentally changing the game — a process I describe in my previous book, *Re-Think: A Path to the Future*.

Today, ten years later, companies still need to change the game if they are going to achieve long-term competitive advantage. And while many of the trends described in *Re-Think* remain the same, now they are playing out at greater speed. Consider how much has changed since 2005. Some of today's ubiquitous products and platforms — Airbnb, Flipkart, the iPhone, Rocket Internet, Twitter, Uber, and Xiaomi — didn't even exist. Others, like 3-D printing, fracking, Facebook, and YouTube, had not yet been commercialized.

I fully expect the next 10-20 years will be just as dynamic as the past 10. Consider the following statement, made in 2014, by one of the founders of *Wired* magazine:

> If we were sent back with a time machine, even 20 years, and reported to people what we have right now and describe what we were going to get in this device in our pocket—we'd have this free encyclopedia, and we'd have street maps to most of the cities of the world, and we'd have box scores in real time and stock quotes and weather reports, PDFs for every manual in the world—we'd make this very, very, very long list of things that we would say we would have and we get on this device in our pocket, and then we would tell them that most of this content was free. You would simply be declared insane. They would say there is no economic model to make this. What is the economics of this? It doesn't make any sense, and it seems far-fetched and nearly impossible. But the next twenty years are going to make this last twenty years just pale. We're just at the beginning of the beginning of all these kind of changes. There's a sense that all the big things have happened, but relatively speaking, nothing big has happened yet. In 20 years from now we'll look back and say, "Well, nothing really happened in the last 20 years."[1]

Fundamental to this dynamic change is innovation. That means new technologies, but also new products and new business models. The cumulative effect of this innovation is to shake up how companies — and individuals — need to operate if they are going to stay competitive in the global marketplace. What's exciting — and sometimes intimidating — is that the pace of innovation has been steadily accelerating. Indeed, it "has never been shorter," as a writer for the *New York Times Magazine* has pointed out.

> An African hand ax from 285,000 years ago, for instance, was essentially identical to those made some 250,000 years later. The

Sumerians believed that the hoe was invented by a godlike figure named Enlil a few thousand years before Jesus, but a similar tool was being used a thousand years after his death. During the Middle Ages, amid major advances in agriculture, warfare and building technology, the failure loop closed to less than a century. During the Enlightenment and early Industrial Revolution, it was reduced to about a lifetime. By the 20th century, it could be measured in decades. Today, it is best measured in years and, for some products, even less.[2]

Just as important, innovations are being adopted rapidly, particularly in developing countries, as a 2014 Pew Research report showed. In Kenya, for example, while just 9 percent of adults owned a cell phone in 2002, 82 percent did by 2013. During the same period, Chinese cell phone ownership increased from 50 percent to 95 percent.[3] (By comparison, just 91 percent of American adults own a cell phone.)

Within the United States, the pace at which technologies are being adopted is also accelerating, as the following chart makes clear.[4]

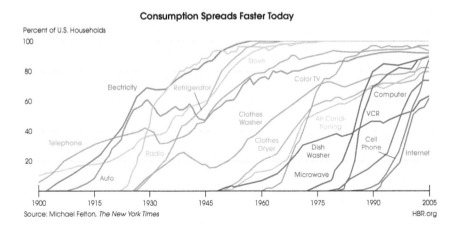

Consumption Spreads Faster Today

Percent of U.S. Households

Source: Michael Felton, *The New York Times*   HBR.org

Amid these changes, global economic integration continues, but with different characteristics. For the first time in human history, more people now live in cities than in rural areas. A larger share of the global population is middle class than ever before. And developing economies are generating a greater share of outbound foreign investment than ever before. But the outlook is also for slower economic growth than what was seen during the boom years in the second half of the 1990s and 2003-2007. And there's evidence that the volume of trade is declining.

These forces, coupled with others, makes it incumbent upon CEOs and business leaders to pursue opportunities, and manage their enterprise, using new and more nuanced approaches.

Growing Global: Lessons for the New Enterprise is focused on helping business and societal leaders understand these changing social and economic dynamics. It offers insights about how the world has changed and where it is trending over the next 10 years. Lessons for enhancing enterprise agility and productivity are brought forth by accomplished global leaders affiliated with The Center for Global Enterprise (CGE).

Shelly Lazarus, the former worldwide CEO of Ogilvy & Mather, writes about the changes sweeping through the world of branding. She says that even amid the incredible diversity of languages, living standards, cultures, and beliefs spread across the world's seven billion people, it's possible to develop a global brand — but only if at its core the company's brand projects a universal truth. It's critical for companies to identify their "promise" of who they are and what they want to be known for.

Doug Haynes, president of Point72 Asset Management and a former director at McKinsey, says that shaping culture positively should be a pressing management matter for all types of companies, and especially so for those engaging customers and clients around the world. He cites a number of reasons why culture matters. This includes its ability to define an enterprise and hold it together across regions, businesses, and generations; and its importance for new business models, such as platform companies.

Chris Caine, president of CGE, and IBM's former vice president for governmental programs, points out that the sheer size of the world's governments, and their reach, makes it vitally important for leaders of every company — regardless of country, size, and industry — to develop a management point of view about their relationship with the public sector. He explains how companies can optimize their relations with governments, what kind of organization is needed to optimize the management resources devoted to dealing with government, and the importance of building trust with government officials.

David Kappos, the former director of the U.S. Patent and Trademark Office, observes that in an era marked by information and content always being available and transparent, innovators must be prepared to play offense and defense with their IP assets. That means seeking patents for innovations and ensuring these patents are enforced in a climate marked by widespread infringement. For that reason, he expects IP disputes will continue to play a prominent — and pivotal — role across the world's economic and legal landscape during the next 10 years. Indeed, the stresses on the IP system will likely escalate, for a simple reason: technology is going to make it easier and easier to share and copy products, and laws preventing new forms of copying (like all laws) lag behind technological progress.

Jean-Pascal Tricoire describes how Schneider Electric, where he serves as chairman and CEO, has transformed its supply chain — changing it from a cost center to a source of competitive advantage, for the company and its customers. The company has embedded strategic thinking supply chain leaders into the different lines of business, which he says has helped to increase customer satisfaction and drive topline growth. He also describes how their focus on developing talent, and promoting a learning culture across the organization, played a key role in the transformation effort.

Jerry Yang, the co-founder of Yahoo!, describes the disruptive innovations of today and tomorrow, and emphasizes the importance of CEOs being relentless in pursuit of a vision for improving the customer experience through innovation. He says that simply expecting innovators to deliver breakthroughs is risky. Successful business leaders need to construct and nurture an innovative mindset enterprise-wide and to have the management fortitude to pivot away from their original vision if market forces dictate.

Peter Evans, a vice president at CGE and former director of GE Corporate's global strategy and analytics team, writes about how companies today are operating in a transformative period, with new digital technologies, coupled with larger and more complex networks (both physical and digital), revolutionizing the way companies innovate and operate. He projects that the forces of change that have been gathering over the past decade are likely to intensify in the decade ahead. As a result, management teams are going to need to rethink their traditional approaches and practices, including their strategies, business models, leadership, core capabilities, value creation and capture systems, as well as organizational structures, if they are going to achieve long-term competitiveness.

Michael Spence, a recipient of the Nobel Prize in Economics, and *Kevin Warsh*, a former Federal Reserve governor, write about the shortfall in U.S. capital investment and the challenges facing China as it transitions to middle-income status. They emphasize the need for business leaders to develop a comprehensive understanding of economic trends — local, national, regional, and global — and engage with policymakers to press for overdue reforms.

In a chapter focused on automation and the workplace, I explore a number of issues that are arising amid the technology-driven changes to the labor market, with a particular focus on key management priorities that can help companies navigate through this era of fast-paced, technology-induced change.

My co-authors and I have chosen to contribute to *Growing Global* because we see comprehensive changes sweeping across the business and economic landscape and we hold a deep desire to help leaders of today and tomorrow on two fronts: to meet the challenges presented by those changes but also to move quickly to seize the extraordinary opportunities they present. Put differently, to seize the future instead of being constrained by it.

We hope our insights and recommendations that follow can help you better understand the age in which we are living, how to navigate it, and how to realize maximum benefit from it.

Beyond Translation

Shelly Lazarus

In the global era, companies face a fundamental question: Can they have a truly global brand? Many people say it's not possible, citing the incredible diversity of languages, living standards, cultures, and beliefs spread across the world's seven billion people. I disagree. If, at its core, a company's brand projects a universal truth, it can be done. While this isn't easy, as there are many management aspects to understand and execute, once achieved, the returns to the business are exponential. Think of companies like American Express, Apple, Dove, Mercedes-Benz, Nestle, Nike, Samsung, and Toyota. The same brand greets you wherever you go in the world. These brands have successfully identified their own universal truths — truths that are so universal they are beyond translation.

Over the years my work with firms has revealed a number of management factors that arise as a company journeys to establish a global brand. Like many of life's endeavors, the most important step is the first. It's critical for companies to identify their "promise" of who they are and what they want to be known for. Without this first act of conviction, all other steps to succeed are for naught.

In the pages ahead I identify a number of management considerations and challenges connected to building and maintaining global brands, including changes across — and misconceptions about — the advertising and marketing sectors. I also take a look at the challenges I see looming large over the next decade.

The Change I've Seen

As companies work to build their brands globally, they are buffeted by on-going evolutions and disruptions across the advertising and marketing landscape. Like many areas of commerce, the disruptions are frequently provoked by new technologies.

One of the biggest changes I've seen during my career is in the very definition of advertising. Traditionally, the definition has been pretty simple: selling something — a product, service, idea, etc. — through mass media (print, TV, radio, billboards). Today, however, due to the ubiquitous nature of information and access to it, advertising is everything and everywhere.

One of the newest areas of focus for creators is integrating advertising into editorial content — what's sometimes called "branded content" or "native advertising." For example, creators can write a story about a brand, or get a product weaved into a TV show or a series, and it is advertising — extremely effective advertising, in fact, when done well. In December 2014, the then-advertising columnist for *The New York Times*, Stuart Elliott, deemed this to be one of the biggest changes in the advertising industry over the past 25 years.[1]

We're also seeing changes in the way advertising is bought and delivered. In India, there is a huge mobile telephone subscriber base, totaling about one billion subscribers. Mobile ads have adapted to a distinctive behavior among the country's consumers. Individuals have a habit of communicating with each other by placing a call and then disconnecting before the recipient has answered, so as to conserve the minutes in their calling plans. The "missed call" phenomenon led a start-up called ZipDial to offer companies the ability to reach customers with text messages that includes a phone number they can call for special offers. Once the call is placed, it disconnects almost immediately, but in return the consumer receives the special offer. Since ZipDial's founding in 2010 (by an American woman who once worked in international marketing for eBay), the company has generated more than 400 million calls. Among the companies who have used the service to reach consumers are Gillette, Disney, and Procter & Gamble. In January 2015, ZipDial was acquired by Twitter.

Another change relates to customer segmentation. It used to be that marketing and advertising were targeted to broad demographic groups by placing ads in the relevant outlets: the *Wall Street Journal* for business types, *Vogue* for the fashion-conscious, etc. While that targeting still exists, it's now possible to be infinitely more precise, thanks to consumers spending more of their time online, which enables the collection and analysis of their viewing, reading, and clicking habits. That information is being deployed to create highly-specific advertising and marketing that is likely to be based on not just individual consumers' online activity, but also their age, gender, income, educational background, spending patterns, marital status, and numerous other pieces of biographical information. Companies are using clever partnerships to engage in targeted marketing of their products to consumers. A few years ago, Pantene, a shampoo brand, joined with the Weather Channel to direct ads to people for different hair products based on the real-time weather where they live.

This laser beam-like marketing has taken on renewed importance as consumers have been accessing content via multiple platforms and, in the case of television, across hundreds of channels. Fragmentation has dramatically escalated in recent years, which makes it much more difficult for marketers using traditional methods to deliver their messages. Stepping into the gap have been entities such as Videology, a New York-based company with a presence in 28 countries. It draws on data derived from billions of transactions to help get the right ad in front of the right person at the right time and in the right context. This information is being coupled with new technology that enables customized television ads to be delivered to individual households. Thus next-door neighbors viewing the same show at the same time on the same channel would see different ads, based on their different consumer profile. This "market of one" is something advertisers could only dream about in the past.

While these disruptions across the advertising and marketing landscape are influencing global branding campaigns, there are some fundamental truths connected to building and managing global brands that management needs to remember and develop processes around. The goal is to harness the positive advantages of the ongoing dynamics and disruptions to drive global growth for the enterprise.

Truth #1:   There is no one model for driving a global brand.

My experience with building brands around the globe has taught me that there are many successful approaches to driving a global brand. Given the many different variables, such as the nature of the brand, its ambitions, opportunities, the corporate structure, the inherent values and culture of the company, as well as budgets, there is no one "right" way.

At one extreme is the "issue orders from headquarters" model. In this case, all marketing communications are created centrally, and then shipped throughout the world for translation into local languages. At the other extreme is a highly localized model where individual markets define the brand locally and each country markets the brand in its own way with minimal contact with headquarters.

Whether the structure is centralized or local, what's most important is for the model to be made explicit. Everyone in the company needs to understand and buy in — and then work to maintain the brand's core message and integrity. Expending energy arguing over who makes the decisions is not only non-productive, it's enervating.

Truth #2:   A brand can serve as a powerful organizing principle.

In the not-so-distant past, global brands were typically talked about in the context of global advertising campaigns. Today, people recognize that brands are so much more than advertising — they represent how a company, product, or service is presented to the public in its entirety. And it's critically important for there to be consistency across geographies. A brand that's focused on service can't offer exemplary service in one country and mediocre service in another. Companies must decide on what their brand will represent and insist on some level of consistency wherever the brand is marketed. Great brands serve as organizing principles. They are big ideas that will require top-level management attention and ownership.

An example of an iconic global brand that serves as the company's organizing principle is American Express. People know what to expect from the company: Consistent quality and service — everywhere in the world. Everything that American Express says and does, regardless of the era and the country, emphasize the same values — customer commitment, quality, integrity, teamwork, personal accountability. Every employee is trained to embody those values anywhere in the world.

For every company operating across borders and cultures, there is a management challenge to ensure operating consistency and brand consistency. There is a constant need to understand how people ingest the brand — and to understand that it's not just one thing that shapes the perception of a brand; it's everything. Once companies accept this, and understand what they're promising, they also need to exercise oversight to ensure that there is operating consistency to how the brand is presented and how it is brought to life. The brand defines a company's culture and it also acts as a control mechanism when expanding into new markets.

Imagine how much more important and challenging this will be for the thousands of platform companies that have been and will be created around the world.

In the case of new companies like Uber and Airbnb, their brands are at the mercy of thousands of contractors and commentators who may not have any particular loyalty to them — and may not even know what the brand represents. Uber has learned this lesson the hard way, with the company being blamed when contract drivers have been charged with a variety of offenses, from rape to reckless driving. For any company whose value is measured at every moment by actual consumer experience, the daily exposure is enormous. The need for management to prioritize educating the network of contractors about the company's values and expectations is critical. The management challenge is infinitely greater than it is for long-established, well-respected, and more traditionally structured, global companies. How the new wave of platform businesses will deal with this need for managing global operating consistency will be an important story foreshadowing the success of such contemporary business models.

Truth #3:   In building global brands, who and how are more important than where.

Getting the right people is the number one issue when working to build a global brand. What does this mean? What kind of people? In my experience, curious, open-minded listeners who are able to tolerate change, uncertainty, and messy organizational structures are most successful in stewarding a global brand. The "best of breed" are problem solvers *who* have an ability to share and think across borders. They are people with an ear for consumer insight. They must believe they can learn from anyone, anywhere, and at any time. The reverse is also true: they should not be narrow-minded, turf-conscious, and entirely focused on their own geography.

The "how" questions are tricky . . . but they must be answered. How is work initiated? *How* does it get approved? What's the role of the "company Center?" Is a comment from the Center a suggestion or an order? It is important that the Center be seen as adding value, not functioning as the police.

Let's take a look at some practicalities. The tough management questions are:

- *How* do you give structure but leave flexibility?

- *Where* do you leave room for interpretation? Do you at all?

- *How* far will you let people go?

- *How* will you know what's happening around the world?
  Do you care?

Being both fair and transparent are important. Distance creates suspicion. Global leaders must not only make decisions, but give some transparency around why decisions are being made. People need to understand why a tough call was made. It's essential to building trust and creating a high-performing team with a culture for excellence and consistency.

Make no mistake, the obligation is squarely on company leaders to decide what is right for their brands and their company. Unfortunately, many leaders leave the "how" undefined. They are often fearful of inhibiting creativity, and want to leave room for the unorthodox idea that is unexpected but brilliant. While brilliant breakout creativity is always laudable, a lack of direction can be torture for everyone involved. It could be one reason why the average tenure of chief marketing officers is less than four years, according to a survey by Spencer Stuart, the executive recruiting firm.[2]

Truth #4: The best brand ideas will leave room for local interpretation.

While a company CEO must be the brand steward (which I discuss in more detail later), that doesn't mean all ideas about the brand must come from the Center. People on the ground should be empowered to shape the expression of the brand for local interpretation — while never touching the core, which is the universal truth!

Today, I'm seeing individual countries being given more flexibility to interpret and implement ideas for their own geography and culture. They're moving beyond translation and helping determine how to maximize the impact of core messages in regional and country markets.

One of the keys to finding this management sweet spot is to set guardrails. The purpose is to get the right people working on the right tasks with the right level of freedom. Managers must make clear where there is room for local invention and experimentation (e.g. local sponsorships, something affecting a local channel or distribution, or local products). Not being explicit about the right balance between central and local intervention risks having people in country markets unnecessarily frustrated. It is singularly unproductive when people in local markets come to believe their ideas about local interpretation will be rejected, and in turn shut down any valuable local insights. Why would you try if you know "it's just going to be killed at headquarters"?

Truth #5:   Be sure to market to local differences that are big and significant.

For local interpretation to be tolerated, if not encouraged, management (both central and local) must market to the big, meaningful differences. An example of a big difference would be market conditions. If a company is a market leader in one country or region but not another, the branding will essentially be the same but the marketing plan and the way it's executed might be completely different. An interesting example is Buick, an American car produced by General Motors. While it is viewed as an antiquated brand in the U.S., it has become a market-leading brand in China. It has the cache of being a foreign car and it is targeted at business executives and government officials, who are big buyers of Buick mini-vans. This is a *big* difference.

Another example is the fast-food chain KFC (formerly known as "Kentucky Fried Chicken"), which though started in the U.S., in Kentucky in fact, has been very successful in China thanks to its focus on localization. The franchise has always been positioned in China as part of the local community and it has been portrayed not as a fast-food option but rather a family dining experience. Each KFC is about twice the size of a typical unit in the U.S., to allow for bigger kitchens and to provide space for customers to dine in and linger. KFC also offers a much wider menu choice — typically 50+ items compared with about 30 in the U.S. — and it offers distinctly Chinese delicacies such as congee (a savory gruel), which is KFC's best-selling breakfast item across China. China is currently KFC's largest market, perhaps because it never stops being KFC, but has adapted in myriad ways to local tastes and culture.

Truth #6:   Speed is good; resolve is better.

In this hyper-connected era, it's tempting to think that a global brand can be built overnight — or at least much, much faster than in the past. Not quite.

The reality for the vast majority of companies is that while the process of building a global *identity* is happening at an accelerated pace, it still takes a very long time to build a global *brand*. The great global brands have typically been decades in the making — and it's a never-ending process. Conditions change, customers change, and competitors change. Brands need to be able to adapt to these changes — all while maintaining a consistent operating performance and universal theme. Great brands evolve constantly.

Unfortunately, brands in today's world *can* be tarnished at the speed of light, for the simple reason that anything that happens, virtually anywhere in the world, can be read, captured, stored or seen globally in an instant — a byproduct of the access to the World Wide Web, driven especially by mobile technology. All of this simply underscores the importance of staying true to the brand and the importance of constant monitoring around the globe. Given that there is no more important asset a company has than its brand, constant resolve is required. Never stop paying attention. Never blink.

Truth #7:   Don't assume success in one market will drive global adoption.

In 2011, Coke created a brilliant idea for personalizing the Coke experience in Australia. The idea was to print popular first names on millions of bottles as a social invitation to find the names of friends and family and encourage them to connect and "Share a Coke." This was the first time Coca-Cola had made such a major change to its packaging — and it worked. While the promotion was underway, Coca-Cola experienced a seven percent increase in sales among young adults in Sydney.

A similar naming campaign followed in the United States, and it was a social media sensation, generating more than half a million Instagram posts. It was also credited with increasing sales two percent — a significant gain, given that the Coke sales had been declining for 11 consecutive years.[3]

What's interesting is that the U.S. campaign did not get underway until 2014 — three years after the Australia campaign. Why it took so long is a mystery, but it's a reminder that success in one country won't necessarily be replicated in other countries. In order to do so, managers have to deal with the practical management realities of execution in order to drive marketing success through a global network. One way to do this is to reward *adaptors* as much as initiators. Recognize the people who apply the great ideas of others. They gain speed and reduce risk. They deserve applause and reward.

By February 2015, Coke's naming campaign had been introduced in about 80 countries — and had been a big success everywhere. How long will it take for the campaign to be launched in the other 120 countries where Coke is sold is yet to be seen. This example suggests that if the Center sees success in one geography, they have to actively move the idea around the world. One can't just assume that this will happen naturally.

Truth #8: It all boils down to partnership and trust.

The global enterprise today takes on many shapes and structures. But no matter what the structure, leaders must remember that their colleagues throughout the enterprise are the most important constituency in building a global brand. Leaders can never talk too much to their people, as they build and deliver the brand from the inside out. Internal audiences spread the joy — to business partners, customers, communities, and regulators, throughout the world. If leaders can identify the true brand leaders, and invest real authority in them, it won't matter where they are located. What will matter is whether an authentically applied universal truth — a company's core essence — is understood, maintained, and supported by employees and those who personify the brand.

Three Common Misconceptions
about an Age-Old Profession

Just as there are fundamental truths about global branding, there are also a number of misconceptions about advertising and branding. A failure to understand these misconceptions can handicap company leaders as they drive global branding efforts.

The most common misconception is to think that branding and marketing are the same thing as advertising. The reality is that branding and marketing are much bigger and broader. Brands are ultimately built through a lifetime of experiences, not an advertisement. The advertising guru Jerry Bullmore once observed, "Consumers build brands like birds build nests: from scraps and straws they chance upon." Advertising can help lay the foundation for what the customer should expect from that experience, and social media has helped create many more touch points, but they can't substitute for the experience. Consumers' impressions of an airline are shaped by much more than the advertising they see in the media or on billboards. A bad flying experience can't be corrected by even the best advertising.

There must be people identified within the organization who have specific responsibility for creating the entire end-to-end customer experience. Starbucks is a shining example of how a company can build a global brand while doing very little in the way of traditional advertising (it did not run a major advertising campaign until 2009). The company and the brand swept through the United States and the world and changed the definition of coffee and café society. It did so because it is about much more than the coffee — it's about the experience, which includes the cups, the furniture, and the way the "baristas" greet customers. The company's in-house coffee guru was once asked what was most important: the coffee, the stores, or the people. "*Everything matters*," he replied.[4]

Another misconception is that branding and marketing are fully controllable by the manufacturer. In decades past, marketing heads could present their plan for the year and then implement it based on the projected schedule, confident that the communications they created would dominate consumers' impression of the company. Today, companies have to accept that much of their brand impression is being driven by a conversation conducted between others that is essentially global, transparent, and instantaneous. As a result, branding and marketing don't operate in a controlled vacuum. It's a constant flow of communications that happens in real-time. The need for courageous, open-minded employees who possess the mental dexterity that's needed in a highly-fluid environment is obvious.

A third misconception is that a company can transform its brand by hiring a new chief marketing officer (CMO). This reflects a naïve appreciation of how brands — which reside in the hearts and minds of the people who use them — work. Once a brand makes an impression on consumers and becomes well-known, it's quite difficult to change that impression. There have been successful brand transformations, but not many, as companies typically try to achieve a transformation by hiring a new CMO with an order to "change my brand." The often-times frustrating truth is that deeply-held impressions, good or bad, can take years — if not decades — to change.

The Decade Ahead

I see a few things shaping the future environment for brand leaders and their ability to excel in managing globally over the next ten years.

Big data and one-to-one

A dominant challenge of the decade ahead will be making sense of the economic opportunities and management challenges connected to the opportunity of big data. Big data enables micro-target marketing to individuals. Right now, data analytics are expanding exponentially. This will only continue. But how companies deal with this opportunity will differentiate leaders from followers. The shift from macro (one-to-many) to micro (one-to-one) advertising capacity has widened the scope of management challenges. Specifically, advertisers will need to figure out how to benefit from customizing advertising to a targeted "market of one."

One of the primary issues with micro-targeting is creating local relevance. While there are some themes that resonate globally, there are many more cultural, regional, and economic differences that need to be integrated into the actual selling of a product or service locally. A company could create a campaign that wins awards globally for the sale of a brand of detergent and run it in India, but if the detergent isn't affordable, relatively few people in India will buy it.

Micro-targeting must be translated into micro-marketing, encompassing pricing, packaging, and the entire customer experience. As new automated search technologies come online they are increasingly delivering precise results; but the insights about how to customize by segment, by geography, or by person are anything but automatic.

Another set of issues relates to how information should be presented on the small screen of a smart phone or an equivalent device. Today, approximately 75 percent of online advertising spending is devoted to banner ads. While few consumers are fond of these ads, I suspect they're still the dominant advertising vehicle because there are few other viable alternatives (and the advertising industry knows how to create them).

A lot of learning will take place over the next few years in this area, but the enterprises leading the way will be those that ensure the "micro" and the "macro" capabilities are integrated. This integrated approach will be the management gold standard whereby the brand sets the context, value, and meaning of the brand, which in turn is translated, made relevant, and delivered individually to each customer or prospect in the world.

Finding talent for contemporary times

For companies and for ad agencies, one of the challenges will be to rethink who to hire and who to advance in this new age. Beyond finding people who are excited by change and challenged by the unknown, we now need engineers and techies all through the marketing ranks. We also need "data scientists," and people with expertise in search engine technology. Marketing departments and advertising agencies are getting increasingly geeky by necessity. In the best environment, the right brains and the left brains are provoking and challenging each other.

Perhaps the most critically important thing will be understanding that *everyone* in the industry is in a continuous learning mode. The focus needs to be on experimentation and a willingness to be wrong. Indeed, if companies are not making some mistakes, it suggests they're not really experimenting. This is the time for people who love complexity, and those who embrace ambiguity as opportunity.

Having an "attuned ear"

Here is a question for all company leaders: Are you listening to what's being said about your company? Social media has changed the corporate landscape — probably forever. Social media has given individual consumers a megaphone that amplifies what they say about companies — whether favorable or unfavorable. Companies can't control this conversation, but they need to know what's being said about them. That's not particularly difficult, though a striking number of companies are unaware of their standing in social media. More challenging will be figuring out how to engage a conversation in ways that steer it in a positive direction, but to do so authentically and without alienating either critics or supporters.

CEO ownership

In the best-managed companies in the world, it's the CEO who takes responsibility for the brand. In an era in which all the communications and points of contact about a company get fragmented, the brand is going to be increasingly important — indeed, it may well be the only thing that holds everything together. Brand focus will be essential regardless of what products or services a company is selling. A brand, in most cases, is the most valuable asset a company has. The CEO *should* be the owner. While marketing functions will certainly still be important, it's the CEOs who will have to set the tone and ensure that brand management is baked into the DNA of the companies they lead, just as finance, compliance, and other core functions are today. The brand gives context to everything the company does.

Jeff Immelt, the CEO of GE, has written about his role as a brand steward:

> Our brand is worth close to $50 billion. That's real money. Every decision I make must support the long-term health of our brand . . .
> It must trump other shorter-term considerations. Few others in the company have as broad, or as passionate, a point of view on this as the CEO. Working together, we tell a meaningful GE story to the world.[5]

Conclusion

A company's brand is its most valuable asset and can provide the most leverage when pursuing new initiatives — regardless of whether these initiatives are customer-facing or internally-focused. But as business leaders contemplate how their company will be branded, they need to ask two fundamental questions: What is the *inherent promise* of our brand? *And* what do we *want* it to be?

Working to craft thoughtful answers to these questions is a critical first step in the development of a global brand. Even amid all of the changes sweeping the advertising and marketing landscape, the fundamental ingredient in building a global brand hasn't changed — it still must speak to a truth that is so universal that it is beyond translation. It must be based on a powerful idea and a particular point of view. As much as everything has changed in the world of marketing, advertising, and brand building, this will never change. For leaders focused on developing a global brand, identifying that universal truth and staying true to it throughout the world is an investment that will pay dividends in perpetuity.

Company Culture: The Foundation for Lasting Performance

Douglas D. Haynes

The concept of "company or enterprise culture" invites challenging questions: What defines culture? Can you use it to achieve other objectives? Can you design it or must it emerge on its own? What is the relationship between enterprise culture and a company's brand? Can you change an enterprise's culture once it is defined? Can you fix it if it is dysfunctional? Do new types of businesses, for example platform companies like Facebook, require new types of cultures?

I appreciate the importance of these questions. For more than two decades, I enjoyed the privilege of consulting to management teams around the world. Over that time, I heard everything one can imagine about culture — from devotees of its importance to doubters of its relevance. Across hundreds of meetings, thousands of hours, and millions of miles, I have come to believe this: culture can inspire employees to levels of performance higher than they imagined or drive a downward spiral of underperformance and cynicism.

Shaping culture positively should be a pressing management matter for all types of companies and especially so for those engaging customers and clients around the world. If doing so is not already your priority, the rest of this chapter offers my views on seven reasons for making it so.

1. Culture is the attractive force that defines an enterprise and holds it together across regions, businesses, and generations.

2. Defining and maintaining culture is an obligation, not an option, for a company's leadership.

3. Successful executives take specific actions to design, mobilize, protect, and reinforce company culture.

4. Leaders change culture — unavoidably — with their words and actions and leaders must adapt culture to changes inside and outside their enterprise.

5. Revitalizing culture is essential for transforming enterprise performance.

6. Culture will be more important than ever for new business models, such as platform companies.

7. The tactics for effective cultural leadership will change over the next five years amid a move toward greater information transparency, availability, and communication.

Culture is a force at the intersection of mission, values, and motivation

Business borrows the word "culture" from the study of societies. What makes up culture in a society? Language? Laws? Behavioral norms? Art? Food? Shared narratives? Rituals? The answer is that no single characteristic defines societies, but the characteristics I have listed define the intersection of many of them. Historically, societies formed around location. High costs of communication and travel, in the forms of risk, time, and resources, forced people to develop defining characteristics together. Today, easy travel and effortless communication allow societies to form around shared interests and across geographic boundaries in ways profoundly different than in other times in history. This offers great potential for companies to define themselves, rather than being defined by where they operate or originate.

Culture is the force that defines enterprises. An enterprise combines financial, human, and intellectual capital to create value for its stakeholders. The nature of the value it creates — its mission — attracts owners, employees, and customers. The mission and the principles by which the enterprise operates — its values — attract customers and employees and earn the enterprise the right to operate within society. The net balance of financial, developmental, and emotional rewards — its motivation — attracts and retains employees. These forces of attraction form the enterprise and maintain the gravitational pull that holds it together. In turn, company culture acts as the force of attraction and retention between owners, employees, and customers of an enterprise.

Culture is an obligation, not an option

"Lasting performance" sounds promising — it's the dream of most managers. But that performance will last only as long as the business leader has the discipline to cultivate the company's culture.

Weak executives neglect, or even exploit, the equity built into their firm's culture in pursuit of short-term solutions or seductive opportunities. For those managers lucky enough to inherit a strong culture, it can seem like an asset that requires little maintenance or something that can be "harvested." They believe that the deep-rooted feel of positive cultural attributes will restore itself despite a little "self-imposed drought of management attention." They are wrong.

Comparing two companies might illustrate the challenge of reinforcing, versus harvesting, a strong culture. IBM and Hewlett-Packard (HP) entered the new millennium in similarly strong positions. After its near-death experience in the beginning of the 1990s, IBM had come back strong under the leadership of Lou Gerstner. HP seemed to have gone from strength to strength in the

1990s tech boom. Before the dot-com bubble burst, both companies appeared poised to lead the enterprise technology industry. By the end of 2010, IBM had increased its revenue to $100 billion, up from $87.5 billion in 1999, while HP had stumbled through the decade, leaving shareholders with a company worth less than it had been twelve years earlier. What happened? Both firms enjoyed strong legacy cultures. IBM's leaders refined and reinvested in theirs. HP's leaders strained theirs past its ability to recover.

IBM has been a mostly organically-built enterprise with a strong sense of identity amongst its employees, who refer to themselves as "IBMers." Soon after becoming CEO in 2003, Sam Palmisano launched a company-wide online brainstorming effort to modernize the company's values statement. He made a commitment to reinvesting in IBM's culture, apparent internally and externally. His predecessor, Lou Gerstner, also emphasized the importance of culture and the need to adapt it to reflect changes inside and outside the workplace. In his memoir, *Who Says Elephants Can't Dance?*, he observed, "I came to see… that culture isn't just one aspect of the game — it is the game." Palmisano said something similar on the company's 100th anniversary in 2011. Referring to the father-son team of Thomas Watson Senior and Junior, who led IBM for a combined 57 years, Palmisano stated, "As bold and visionary as both were, their greatest innovation or contribution was a culture or a way of doing things."

HP, like IBM, prioritized culture in its early years. Here's how Jim Collins, author of the best-selling book *Good to Great,* described HP's culture, as set out by its founders, William Hewlett and David Packard:

> Hewlett and Packard rejected the idea that a company exists merely to maximize profits. "I think many people assume, wrongly, that a company exists simply to make money," Packard extolled to a group of HP managers on March 8, 1960. "While this is an important result of a company's existence, we have to go deeper to find the real reasons for our being." He then laid down the cornerstone concept of the HP Way: *contribution.* Do our products

offer something unique — be it a technical contribution, a level of quality, a problem solved — to our customers? Are the communities in which we operate stronger and the lives of our employees better than they would be without us? Are people's lives improved because of what we do? If the answer to any of these questions is "no," then Packard and Hewlett would deem HP a failure, no matter how much money the company returned to its shareholders.[1]

The "HP Way" endured for decades, permeating everything the company did and helping make it an early emblem of Silicon Valley ingenuity and success.

But the HP Way gradually frayed. As an HP consultant wrote in the company's own magazine in 1998, "I am finding less and less identification with that core ideology [the HP Way]. Many people seem distanced from it, and many really aren't aware of the business rationale behind it: to serve society through technology, to dominate chosen market segments, and to make a fair profit." This consultant pointed out that the company had 130,000 employees and that "without leaders to pass on a core ideology . . . the legacy dies. I am concerned that the legacy seems to be flickering."[2]

The consultant's concerns proved prescient. HP's acquisition of Compaq in 2002 and EDS in 2008 resulted in a prolonged struggle to integrate three very large, very different companies and cultures. HP replaced its CEO in 2005. It became embroiled in a boardroom scandal that sparked several resignations — including the Chair of the Board of Directors. An investigation by the U.S. government followed. Another controversy, involving personal misconduct on the part of the CEO, led to his resignation. Leadership of Hewlett-Packard changed hands four times from 2005 to 2011. The fabric of HP's culture — the HP Way — was lost.

I do not compare IBM and HP over this period to imply that one culture is "good" and the other "bad." I compare them to illustrate the pervasive power of culture as a foundation for performance. Two companies, similarly positioned, competing in the same markets for the same customers, with comparably enviable positions entering the year 2000, diverge dramatically in the ensuing decade. The difference can be found in the attention paid to culture by the leaders of IBM. In the 18 years that Lou Gerstner and Sam Palmisano led IBM, reinvesting in the firm's culture remained a top priority. I enjoyed the privilege of working closely with Sam and his leadership team through his tenure as CEO. They recognized that the responsibility to adapt, refine, and reinforce IBM's culture began, and ended, with them. They understood that a culture left to drift, to emerge and evolve on its own, would dissipate.

Five actions for cultivating your company's culture

Companies are complex organisms. Every time I thought that I had found "the answer" regarding how they work, I found a new set of questions. Understanding large, global enterprises offers, and demands, a lifetime of study. I don't claim to have found "the answer" by any stretch; however, I have learned five actions to design and cultivate culture within a company.

1. Start with the stakeholders

Leaders can design the culture that they intend; in fact, they must. A company culture left to "emerge" or define itself is as likely to produce weeds as it is wildflowers. Farmers looking to make their land productive must first understand the potential and limits of the land. A leader looking to grow a productive culture must first understand the stakeholders, particularly the owners, and customers.

Owners define the solution space for designing culture. Privately-owned companies may enjoy freedom from short-term, period-based performance pressure. At the same time, they must respect the appetite of their owners for risk, capital investment, and involvement. Publicly-owned companies may enjoy greater capacity for bold investment, but accept that it comes with constant inspection. Companies owned by governments, in whole or part, serve a broad constituency of interests and may be subject to objectives that shift with political regimes. Leaders of startup companies often begin with the notion that they have no limits imposed by owners; in fact, they often choose an entrepreneurial path to free themselves from those limits. It works . . . until they need capital. Venture funders usually accompany their cash with expectations and requirements — their own solution space for culture. When a startup reaches time for its initial public offering — the event that its founder(s) work toward for years — the next set of expectations arrive with public funding. In every case, the leaders must weigh the opportunities and limits that come with its owners when designing the intended culture.

Leaders must understand the nature of their "ideal employees" or role models when defining the culture they intend. Like owners, they come with opportunities and limits. Leaders should start by determining the employees who are most critical to the company's success. For example, a manufacturing company might center its culture on operations management and sales talent. A hospitality company might pivot around front-line service delivery personnel. A professional services firm must revolve around client-facing team leaders.

Leaders must then determine the type of people they want in those critical roles. For example, a professional services firm might want deep subject matter experts. The type of person who builds deep expertise over a career may have different wants and needs than a multi-faceted generalist. IKEA, the highly successful Swedish furniture maker and retailer, emphasizes its culture during recruiting. They state that, "We don't just want to fill jobs; we want to partner with people. We want to recruit unique individuals who share our values. Co-workers are not restricted in IKEA; we listen and support each individual to identify his or her needs, ambitions, and capabilities."

Leaders must determine the employee value proposition that resonates with their ideal employee. What motivates them? What inspires them? What irritates or frightens them? Leaders can't afford to assume they know the answers. I retired from consulting at the end of 2013 and became president of an asset management firm.[3] Conventional wisdom held that investment professionals were motivated solely by money. I interviewed the firm's portfolio managers and thought I heard something more. With the help of Vega Factor,[4] a startup consulting firm specializing in organization culture and motivation, we surveyed the entire company, including a section on personal and professional motivation. Compensation does motivate our investment professionals; however, it ranks third, not first, among their sources of satisfaction. The enjoyment from the work of investing — analyzing companies, interpreting market movements, anticipating changes — ranks highest. Professional growth and development — learning and sharpening their craft — ranks second. These two motivators hold even greater importance to our highest performers. The conventional wisdom, in this case, was both incorrect and inconsiderate to our investment professionals. The types of people we want, in the roles most critical to our success, are more motivated by support to perform and develop more than by money alone. They are thoughtful professionals, not heartless mercenaries.

Value proposition, brand, and culture are not separable. Your company's values are instantiated in your employees. Your employees bring your value proposition to life. Your value proposition defines your brand. Over time, your brand defines the customers who choose you over your competitors. When leaders choose the intended culture for their company, they should have a target customer in mind. For consumer companies, the definition might also include an occasion or event. For example, Starbucks aims to serve people when they treat themselves to something special during their day. In that moment, the fifty-something executive and twenty-something graduate student have more in common than demographic information suggests.

2. Design the culture, then adapt it to keep it relevant

In the early years of a company's life, its leaders — often the founding leaders — lay the foundation for culture. Thoughtful leaders take care to define the company's mission and the principles by which it will operate. As the company matures and its challenges change, leaders must adapt the culture to the new context in which it operates.

As an example, Google's founders and early leaders decided to shape its culture deliberately. The company's well-known catchphrase, "Don't be evil," was a precursor to a list of ten principles established to guide the company's development when it was still in its infancy. They are:

- Focus on the user and all else will follow.
- It's best to do one thing really, really well.
- Fast is better than slow.
- Democracy on the web works.
- You don't need to be at your desk to need an answer.
- You can make money without doing evil.
- There's always more information out there.
- The need for information crosses all borders.
- You can be serious without a suit.
- Good just isn't good enough.

Google's leaders took care to design the culture they wanted. As the company grew — spectacularly — and evolved, they recognized the need to refine and adapt the culture to their new context. In March 2015, Google's Senior Vice President of People Operations, Laszlo Bock, published a book that contained another ten-point list. This one offered Laszlo's view, based on Google's continual reinvestment in its culture, on things companies can do to "transform their teams and transform their workplace." They are:

- Give your work meaning.

- Trust your people.

- Hire only people who are better than you.

- Don't confuse development with managing performance.

- Focus on the 'two tails'.

- Be frugal and generous.

- Pay unfairly.

- Nudge.

- Manage the rising expectations.

- Enjoy! And then go back to No. 1 and start again.

Although these lists serve slightly different purposes, you can see the change in Google's challenges by comparing them. In the latter list, Google's leaders pay more attention to the challenges that tend to emerge in more mature companies, such as "managing performance" and "expectations." Laszlo's words show that Google's leaders are adapting, refining, and reinvesting.

3. *Align the business design to intended culture*

I asserted that culture solidifies around aspects of the company that its leaders design and control. What are those aspects? The most important are the operating model, the management system, and the approach to performance management. These are the elements of the company that its employees feel every day.

We can define a company's operating model by its basis for innovation, sources of scale, and points of integration. Innovation requires change and adaptation. Scale requires standards and commonality. The operating model resolves the inherent tension between these two important forces by prescribing where each will take priority. Consider a military organization. Standards seem to dominate the culture — uniforms, ranks, chains of command, and strict adherence to procedure. Dig deeper and you will find that front-line leaders are expected to exercise adaptive and innovative leadership to fulfill their missions in hostile and unpredictable conditions. Where and how the military's leaders adhere to standards and exercise adaptive decision-making shapes the culture of any military organization. In most companies, the defining line between innovation and scale occurs at the point where its leaders choose to optimize performance. Often, the responsibility for this integration resides with a "general manager" or "business leader." Choices around where these points reside in the organization (e.g., local versus global, product versus market) add to the definition of company culture.

The management system provides the architecture for decision-making. Its components include the decision rights for each important role in the organization, the expectations for participation and inclusion in decision-making, and the processes for resolving differences. Again, choices about the management system play a profound role in determining culture. Putting decision rights closer to the front line will make a company more dynamic — and more chaotic. Including more inputs in decision-making adds to cohesion — and reduces speed.

Performance management includes measures, rewards and consequences (financial and non-financial), and the method of inspecting inputs and outputs. Decisions regarding performance management provide the most powerful conduit of company culture for employees. Experiences with performance management — positive and negative — can define employees' careers.

Leaders must align these elements of the company to the culture they intend to develop. All too often, they misalign, or allow these elements to be misaligned, making a mockery of intended values. For example, if the leaders of a company intend to make customer service a priority, they must also make the point of integration in their operating model close to the customer. They must move decision-making close enough to allow those interacting with customers the freedom to address their needs quickly and completely. They must measure customer satisfaction and inspect it at the level of events, not the average (because customers do not experience averages).

Nordstrom, the U.S.-based clothing retailer, and Ritz-Carlton, the upscale hotelier with properties in 29 countries, provide good examples of aligning the management system with their intended culture. The management of both companies puts considerable decision-making power in the hands of front-line customer service leaders. Both companies have earned reputations for exceptional service; in fact, Ritz-Carlton has established a "Leadership Center" that offers courses on customer service to the public.

Measures and rewards often trip up company executives. How often have you heard someone complain that they are asked to do "X" while being measured, and compensated, on "Y"? Changes in strategy without corresponding changes in performance management make employees feel that management is disingenuous, incompetent, or both. The 3M Corporation provides a good example of aligning measures with its intended culture. Headquartered in the U.S. and operating in over 70 countries, 3M describes itself as "a global innovation company that never stops inventing." To reinforce that value, 3M's leaders tie employee bonuses to delivering 30% of revenue from products commercialized within the previous four years. They also believe that "creativity needs freedom." To that end, they have encouraged employees to devote 15% of their time to independent projects — a practice they pioneered and have maintained since 1948. To use a gambling metaphor, compensation is the "table stakes" for rewards — you can lose by getting it wrong, but you cannot win on it alone. Rewards must also include recognition, advancement, and professional development opportunities. In some firms, a paid sabbatical reigns as the highest form of reward for sustained performance.

4. Supplement culture with controls

I have heard culture described as "what your people do when no one is watching." While that might be a good definition, it is not sufficient as a management practice. Interpretation, judgment, and human behavior will always vary, especially across countries and cultures. Training will reduce unwanted variations. Clear standards for behavior and consequences for violating them also help. All these things still will not assure compliance with your company's intended values. Company leaders must take appropriate measures to prevent damaging behavior and be prepared to take action when violations occur.

The most extreme cases take place when individuals betray a hard-earned culture that is central to the company's mission. Arthur Andersen's partners lost their entire firm in 2002 when one of their ranks violated their most fundamental values while serving Enron.

Barings Bank collapsed in 1995 after a single employee racked up trading losses of $1.3 billion. One may be tempted to dismiss these as tragic events — outliers unrelated to culture. I disagree. The damage these events do to the belief that employees, communities, and customers have in an enterprise mandate that company leaders deal with them as part of culture-building. Consider the following questions at the intersection of culture and controls:

- Have you defined standards for behavior — what to do and what not to do — that reinforce your stated values?

- Do you conduct mandatory training, including scenario-based assessments, to ensure your employees can translate your standards into daily decisions?

- How do you monitor the actions of employees to ensure compliance?

- What actions do you take when an employee violates your standards? How are those actions communicated to the rest of the organization?

- What recognition do you give an employee who makes the right choices, especially in ambiguous or difficult circumstances?

Few companies have clear answers for all of these questions. Some managers struggle with the idea of monitoring employee behavior, preferring to trust their people to "do the right thing." These same managers claim shock when they discover — often after years — that an employee has operated outside the firm's values. While it may seem unfair, if someone who reports to you "bends" the firm's rules, your other employees usually assume that you are aware and simply choose not to act. They perceive that the firm's stated values are just slogans, that management isn't serious about them, and that their own behaviors are unappreciated. The situation erodes a positive and cohesive culture. If you are serious about building a strong culture, you can trust but you must verify. On the positive side, when you find employees doing the right things, you have an opportunity to reinforce them through recognition and appreciation. Positive teaching moments are every bit as powerful as negative ones, if you seize them.

5. Own cultural leadership

Gandhi reportedly said, "be the change you wish to see in the world." Leaders must live the values they wish to see in their company's culture. In a defined culture, employees and customers will judge every word and action of the leaders against the articulated mission and values. They will read promotions, new hires, and dismissals as either reinforcing or compromising to the culture. Leaders receive zero "down time" from being assessed. Customers interpret the authenticity of the company's culture based on successes and failures to deliver on the expectations created by value proposition and brand. Failures count more. When customer service breaks down — for any reason — how the company responds defines its culture in the mind of the customer. The ability to engage the customer empathetically, take responsibility, respond decisively, and follow up to ensure satisfactory resolution must be built into the management system and rewarded through performance management. It all traces back to the company's leaders, the thoroughness of their cultural design, and their consistency in cultivating the values they want in their company.

Leaders change culture

The title of this section intentionally offers options for interpretation. The prior section asserted that the actions of an enterprise leader are judged by its stakeholders and, over time, affect culture — unavoidably. This section explains that leadership change triggers cultural change and that successful leaders deliberately change culture when enterprise context shifts.

Leadership change creates discontinuity in company culture. A new leader will be perceived to: a) reinforce the culture by reaffirming its values; b) refine the culture by refining or changing the emphasis amongst its values; or c) disrupt the culture by adjusting the mission, disavowing some values, and/or introducing new values. Owners, employees, and customers may see all three types of cultural impact as positive or negative, depending on the perceived strength and health of the culture at the time of the change. In some ways, *not* changing a strong, healthy culture may be the toughest challenge for a new leader. The whole world seemed to hold its breath when Tim Cook stepped up to lead Apple following the death of Steve Jobs. Would Apple innovate as boldly? Would the developers on the Apple platform maintain their fervent following? These were questions of culture, not competence, for Mr. Cook. Owners, employees, and customers noted every decision and every word — they even noted how he dressed. At the time of this writing, Mr. Cook appears to be passing the test of maintaining Apple's cultural momentum . . . and the world is still watching.

Can enterprise context shift so dramatically that culture must be redefined? Absolutely. The approach I shared earlier has the same impact when adapting a culture as defining it the first time. The leader must start with the stakeholders. As a company matures, its owners may change — or change their expectations of the company. For example, a public company in its growth phase may attract shareholders that value top-line growth more than returns. As the company matures, its ownership may shift to shareholders that value earnings and dividends. An organization that produces earnings through efficient execution cannot have the same culture as the organization with growth as the primary objective. In the same situation, the critical roles may change. The ideal employees for these roles may change to suit the new challenge. If the owners change and the ideal employees change, how can the culture not change?

Effective enterprise leaders keep a pulse on the context of their company and sense the need for change before the forces of stakeholder attraction weaken. Performance itself can signal these shifts. When an enterprise struggles to execute, something has changed for employees. When satisfaction or market share slips, something has changed for customers. When stock prices soften relative to investment alternatives, something has changed for owners. As vital as monitoring these changes seems, enterprise leaders often allow their signals to be drowned out. Successful enterprise leaders make time to listen to their stakeholders, explore the root causes of performance gaps, and assess the context of their enterprise. They catalyze cultural adaptation before its strength and health can erode.

Cultural transformation must lead performance transformation

If we define "culture" as the forces of attraction and retention between owners, employees, and customers of an enterprise, we can define "crisis" as the flight of those stakeholders from the enterprise when those forces fail. Leading an enterprise out of crisis must begin with redefining and rebuilding those forces. The same actions for defining and adapting cultures apply when transforming them. The stakes are just higher.

In crisis, understanding the stakeholders matters even more

Kodak's bankruptcy stands as one of the more heartbreaking failures in American business. In 1970, Kodak was one of the world's most valuable corporations. At its peak, in 1976, Kodak sold 90 percent of all film sold in the United States, and 85 percent of all cameras. By 2005, Kodak was in crisis and gambled the company on a dramatic transformation — that failed. By 2013, restructuring firms were selling off Kodak's patents to salvage whatever value remained.

More than a few explanations exist for Kodak's fall: unwillingness to cannibalize its film business with the digital technologies it created; strategic missteps in failed diversification; inability to reduce costs quickly as technology compressed industry margins. Perhaps the reason lay not in the actions Kodak failed to take, but in the reason Kodak failed to take them — its stakeholders were not committed to the changes required.

One vignette in the story of Kodak's demise illustrates its cultural breakdown. When Kodak announced its digital strategy with its third quarter shareholder communications in 2005, its stock fell about 25 percent in a day. The "no confidence" vote and resulting financial distress sealed the company's fate. How did it happen? By 2005, the majority of Kodak's shareholders owned its stock for the dividend. In fact, the company's leaders and board maintained its rich dividend as its share price eroded over the preceding years, making it the highest dividend yield stock in the market. The announced digital strategy: a) declared new business priorities in consumer electronics, digital displays, and wide-format printing; b) reduced earnings expectations for the near- and medium-term with plans for dramatic reinvestment for new technology and growth; and, c) cut the dividend by 50 percent to redirect cash from shareholders to growth investments. The strategy ignored the interests of one of Kodak's most important stakeholders — its owners. The new strategy rejected the premise they had for owning Kodak stock.

I have personal experience with a different kind of company crisis. At the beginning of 2014, I joined SAC as an in-house advisor to help my friend, Steve Cohen, plot a course to restore his embattled firm. By mid-year, I had signed on as President of his redefined firm, Point72 Asset Management, to lead the firm on that course. While the firm enjoyed strengths one would not imagine from reading about it in the media (e.g., excellent talent in every part of the firm, superior risk management and training capabilities, strong *esprit-des-corps*), it lacked the powerful, positive forces of culture to pull it together. Discovery of employees acting unprofessionally may have eroded the culture they once had. Persistent media assaults may have undermined trust within the firm. The prolonged investigation and lingering scandal may have damaged "permission" between the firm and the communities in which it operates. Whatever the causes, the firm was in crisis.

Looking ahead, the stakeholders shared the same interests. Steve Cohen, the founder and owner, believed that SAC had been a good firm prior to the scandal and wanted to use the event as a shakeup to make it a great firm. When he asked me to join as an advisor, he told me, "I would rather shut it down and walk away than allow it to just survive. We must become a great firm. Everyone who stayed could have left, but they believed in themselves and our firm. They deserve nothing less than an all-out effort to be great." The employees wanted to be proud of their firm again. Jon Weiner, one of the longest-tenured investment professionals told me, "We used to be the best — everyone wanted to work here. We won't be successful if we can't make that true again."

We started by rejecting the recently popular notion that the hedge fund industry is an inherently exploitative business, operating at the fringes of market regulations. In fact, my study of the firm revealed that the highest performing investment professionals succeed through industry expertise, intelligent risk management, objectivity, and discipline. Steve and the management team worked together to define every aspect of Point72's culture, with ethics and integrity at the center. We engaged approximately 250 of our 850 employees to codify it in the form of a statement of mission and values. We defined professional standards well above and more broad than the regulations that govern our industry and trained every employee on their application. We created a new function — surveillance — to verify that the actions of every employee, including Steve and the executive team, adhere to those standards. We took decisive actions any time the standards were breached. Steve and the executive team constantly reinforce our professional standards and view reinforcing them as an obligation of leadership.

Point72 is far from reaching its potential; however, it is building momentum. We are engaged in "all-out effort to be a great firm," beginning and ending with our culture.

New enterprise forms "raise the bar" for culture

"Platform" businesses harness the Internet for immediate, global distribution and tap into network effects across their ecosystem to fuel innovation. Companies like eBay, Facebook, YouTube, LinkedIn, Airbnb, Alibaba, and Uber — to name only a few — have grown and built market value faster than any enterprises in history. At a CEO forum hosted by the Center for Global Enterprise in 2014, Sam Palmisano said "Uber's distribution has already reached almost 50 countries in four years. It took IBM 50 years to do the same." (Uber's distribution is now over 60 countries.) Physical infrastructure building does not constrain the growth of platform businesses. They ride on the existing devices, networks, and IT infrastructure built by other firms, often for other purposes. They are the ultimate "agile" business units, often comprised of little more than product developers and support personnel. Their ecosystems include users who create a large share of their value.

Building culture across such a loosely-organized value chain can be a challenge. Rapid growth and globalization makes that challenge greater. It also makes it more important. Brian Chesky, the founder of Airbnb, a successful platform company that connects people who want to rent rooms, typically for short-term stays, to their customers, wrote in 2014 about the importance of culture:

> Why is culture so important to a business? Here is a simple way to frame it. The stronger the culture, the less corporate process a company needs. When the culture is strong, you can trust everyone to do the right thing. People can be independent and autonomous. They can be entrepreneurial. And if we have a company that is entrepreneurial in spirit, we will be able to take our next "(wo)man on the moon" leap. Ever notice how families or tribes don't require much process? That is because there is such strong trust and culture that it supersedes any process. In organizations (or even in a society) where culture is weak, you need an abundance of heavy, precise rules and processes. [5]

Airbnb's business model rests on developing customer trust: customers are, after all, sleeping in the homes of strangers. Airbnb's leaders believe that fostering a partnership and community among the users (both renters and rentees) will protect the interests of the users and the enterprise.

For Airbnb, culture may or may not be enough to protect those interests and their firm. For Uber, lack of a strong culture that bonds their entire ecosystem has already hurt their business. New York University professor, Arun Sundararajan, has written about the contrasting cultures of Airbnb and Uber. He observes that Airbnb has worked to foster partnership and community while Uber seems determined to place distance between its platform and the providers that use it. He states:

> (Uber's) pricing changes are implemented centrally and announced unilaterally, with no visible provider consultation. Community building is not a priority. A large gathering of Uber drivers is more likely to be a protest than a convention, ironic given the frequency with which taxi drivers stage similar gatherings to advocate a regulatory shutdown of the service, in the U.S. and beyond.[6]

Some see the reported instances of wrongdoing by Uber-affiliated drivers, including allegations of rape and reckless driving, as a byproduct of the company's combative culture. As its leaders are now embroiled in legal battles and barred from operating in many cities, there can be no doubt that its culture has already hindered its growth in some markets.

Culture in a world of extreme transparency and connectivity

In the past, outsiders to an enterprise's culture could only glimpse it. Customers might infer the culture of a company through its product and customer service. Regulators or government officials might develop their perspective through reports or a visit. New recruits might develop a sense through the interview process. No longer. Today, countless online outlets allow current and former employees to share their experiences at specific companies. Some are company-specific blogs for large enterprises. Others are multi-company information clearing houses, like Glassdoor. Online media also offers a point of view on company culture, drawing from the online outlets as well as conventional person-to-person journalism. Enterprise leaders can no longer deal with cultural breaches discretely. The uglier the instance, the faster it will spread and farther it will radiate.

Enterprise leaders of today and tomorrow must do a more thorough job of designing and owning all the elements of culture. In today's world of extreme transparency and connectivity, it is both harder and easier to stay atop of the vitality of your enterprise's culture. Breakdowns at any point in the management system will be known widely. Manager behavior will be scrutinized more closely. Single instances will be amplified to look like persistent patterns. As Shelly Lazarus notes in her chapter on global branding, brands are built every day by a company's behavior. This is also true for a company's culture. It is reinforced or degraded every day by the behavior of its employees.

The same communication technologies that create extreme transparency can indulge shortcuts on the part of enterprise leaders. Executives overwhelmed with a steady flood of emails can be tempted to communicate important cultural messages over the same medium. Human behavioral research shows that we convey over half of our meaning through nonverbal cues, such as posture and facial expression. Verbal cues, like tone, volume, and pauses, convey another large portion of substance. How much meaning can an enterprise leader transmit through email or texts? What are the risks of mixed messages or confusion? Given the speed and lack of control from transparency, how fast and far will a cultural miscommunication move?

No substitute exists for personal interaction when shaping the culture of your enterprise. You don't need to deliver every message face-to-face; however, you do need to keep personal communication central in your efforts to cultivate your intended culture. When you use broadcast email, have a communications professional work with you to ensure the tone and meaning fulfill your objectives. You and your leaders should avoid using technology for critical communications — such as rewarding good behavior or levying consequences for bad behavior. If you must use technology for the sake of speed, use the phone.

When does technology improve cultural leadership? Some technologies dramatically improve the scope and specificity of facts available to enterprise leaders as they design and manage their cultures. Employee and customer input can be gathered faster and with more nuance than ever before. Individual employee behavior can be verified through multiple means. Job performance can be quantified and monitored for almost any role. Consequently, much of the guesswork of cultural leadership can be replaced with information rigor and depth. Investments in these technologies, and the capability to translate their outputs to actions, can yield high returns for enterprise leaders.

Conclusion

The world of business has changed a lot over the past 10 years — a decade that began the extreme operational integration of the global economy. New business models, such as platform companies, have emerged and grown, creating new value for customers and communities alike. We have moved to a more demand-side global economy, where customer choices and behavioral transparency are the new guideposts. In a world such as this, measures of authenticity and reliability are being redefined. Company cultures have always been a characteristic used by customers to make their choices. Today, leaders have greater leverage to share their company culture with their customers and clients to build deeper trust and rapport.

Company leaders, and especially leaders of globally integrated enterprises, must understand the power of culture in today's world. They must develop the skills for cultural leadership. It is an obligation, not an option. Effective cultural leadership requires a deliberate, informed, and thorough approach, starting with stakeholders and touching on the company's operating model, management system, and performance management. Technology offers enterprise leaders better tools than ever before available for informing cultural leadership, while simultaneously "raising the bar" of employee and customer expectations. As Lou Gerstner said, "culture isn't just one aspect of the game . . . it is the game."

A Market Force Like No Other

Christopher G. Caine

D iscussions of global business tend to overlook one very large entity. It has operations everywhere in the world, it collects approximately $17 trillion of revenue, and it employs more than 100 million people. It also devotes more than $400 billion to research and development annually. Its commercial assets constitute the largest pool of wealth in the world — double the world's total pension savings and ten times the holdings of all the world's sovereign wealth funds.[1] Divided into nearly 200 operating units, it has more than seven billion shareholders.

You won't find this entity on the Fortune Global 500 or any other list of the world's largest companies. That's because it's not a company, though it is a market force like no other: government.

The sheer size of the world's governments, and their reach, makes it incumbent upon leaders of every company — regardless of country, size, and industry — to develop a management point of view about their relationship with the public sector. For one-person businesses that only operate domestically and deliver routine services, this viewpoint may not need to extend much beyond ensuring compliance with local regulations and tax codes. At the other end of the spectrum, large enterprises (whether they be publicly traded, private, or state-owned) that operate in multiple countries and multiple industries need a cohesive and informed approach as they face an array of fiscal and regulatory impacts from different governments.

To more fully appreciate government's size and capacity, consider the following from the 2015 Fortune Global 500 rankings: Walmart and Royal Dutch Shell — the two largest publicly-traded and publicly-owned companies — collectively employ about 2.3 million people (with Walmart accounting for 2.2 million of that total). And in the most recent fiscal year, revenue of the two companies totaled about $906 billion.

Now compare that to the governments of the world's two largest economies: China and the United States. Together they employ approximately 38 million people. And their revenues total $8.3 trillion. And from a capacity perspective, consider that in April 2009, amid the financial crisis, then-U.S. Treasury Secretary Tim Geithner indicated that by year end 2010, the United States Government would inject $800 billion into the U.S. economy — nearly the combined size of these two giant enterprises.

Beyond an individual government's size and capacity, there are certain powers only it can exercise. Those powers can be exercised in ways that are extremely beneficial as companies invest and expand (domestically and internationally). Conversely, governments can (and do) exercise powers in arbitrary and unpredictable ways that can be a destructive force to companies. What's important to remember is that governments have the power to create, eliminate, and change markets overnight, if they choose to do so.

In this chapter, I provide recommendations for how companies can optimize their relations with governments, what kind of organization is needed to optimize the management resources devoted to dealing with government, and the importance of building trust with government officials. I will also lay out the basic functions of government and look at how government has been impacted by societal changes over the past 10 years, and how it will likely be impacted over the decade ahead.

Role of government

All governments play the same three roles, regardless of their form, ideological orientation, or scope.

First, all governments are *"rule makers"* — setting public policy and enforcing those policies. This role includes setting rules (i.e. laws, regulations, etc.) for society and an economy. This is not just limited to dimensions of economic activity such as taxation, international trade, intellectual property, the environment, financial markets, and real estate. It also includes the values and behavioral standards a society chooses to establish.

Second, governments are *investors* — allocating public and sometimes private capital (through mandates) to programs ranging from education to transportation to health care to infrastructure. For example, governments make decisions around questions such as: How robust does Internet access and bandwidth need to be? How much should be allocated for healthcare purchases of pharmaceuticals and medical services?

Third, governments are *purchasers* — of goods and services. The U.S. federal government, for example, spends $530 billion on procurement annually, leading it to be christened, "the world's biggest customer." Globally, government procurement accounts for 10-15 percent of every economy's gross domestic product, as estimated by the World Trade Organization.[2]

Given these realities, the implications for companies are profound. Clearly, company leaders need to have an understanding of these roles. How is public policy made? How does government set its priorities? Who are the decision-makers about government investments? What market impact will government behavior have on my sector — my competitors? And what is required in order to be identified as a potential supplier to government?

These and other questions parallel the analysis business leaders go through when deciding to enter commercial markets and activities. Yet many fail to apply the same rigor when it comes to understanding and shaping the behavior of this "market force like no other."

And most important for a company's leaders to remember, like it or not, is that governments grant companies license to operate. And while every company's management desires to operate their enterprise in the manner that they feel will most effectively meet their business objectives, the ability to do this will be directly impacted by governments' willingness to trust the company — trust that is based on whether the company is viewed as delivering societal benefits. Hence, there is an imperative for companies to build trust with government so that the permission it grants management to operate maximizes freedom of action and is more of an accelerator for growth than a barrier to it.

The past 10 years

In his iconic works on globalization, *The Lexus and the Olive Tree* (1999) and *The World is Flat* (2005), Tom Friedman described the structural changes shaping the world, stemming from the accelerating pace of global integration, principally economic integration. These and other works presented a framework for understanding a pace of change that people sensed and felt but hadn't quite grasped. But there was an under-appreciation for an aspect of globalization that would be just as profound — governments around the world and their operations joining the rest of society, online.

Throughout my professional career, the three common roles of government have been carried out in a framework of limited information and hierarchy. Many governments, regardless of form, enjoyed a *de facto* monopoly on the information about their country and its activities. They were frequently deemed to have the most complete and authoritative information. Societies were organized around it. People made decisions from it. Markets valued certain investments over others based upon the information coming from government sources. And most of this information was collected and packaged in an environment of confidentiality and/or secrecy.

Very little of what I've just described is still true. Over the past decade, government information has become much less trusted and deemed less sacrosanct — a byproduct of the world moving into a new age of transparency. This is a profound change — one that I believe will shape how companies interact with government in the years ahead. The other change has been a pause, or some might say a step back, by government policy makers regarding economic openness.

The pervasive and evolving digital domain

The rise of global connectedness among individuals, through the proliferations of smart phones, more robust and pervasive communications and computing networks, cloud computing, and the arrival of the "video internet," have had sweeping implications for governments and companies alike. This represents a seismic change to government's status as the definitive provider of "official information."

With people and companies in virtually every region of the world now capable of being connected with each other on multiple levels, we have entered a new era of transparency. And this transparency has ushered in a new and higher level of organizational and behavioral accountability. Indeed, governments, as well as companies (as referenced in the chapter by Shelly Lazarus), face a technology-enabled and recorded referendum every day on their efficacy and trustworthiness.

Being able to watch videos, on platforms such as YouTube, Tudou, and others, can showcase information refuting the claims of government officials. Technology has also been employed to disseminate confidential information held by governments. Examples include the Wikipedia release of internal messages written by U.S. State Department officials (which revealed the disconnect between the U.S. government's public statements and private deliberations) and Edward Snowden's disclosure of classified documents revealing the U.S. National Security Agency's global surveillance programs.

While episodes like these may not be everyday occurrences, the broader trend of greater transparency poses an enormous challenge for all governments as they seek to build trust and maintain it. If their rhetoric is not aligned with reality, there is a high likelihood their duplicity will be publicized (as Russia's was after claiming it did not have troops or equipment in Ukraine) and their standing at home and/or abroad will suffer.

What we have seen over the last ten years, and will continue to see, is an erosion of trust in government-distributed information. While government information may have been viewed skeptically by some in the past, it now faces unprecedented challenges. Fewer individuals and institutions will consider it to be the most authoritative source, and they will look elsewhere for guidance when making decisions about future activities.

A closing door on global economic openness

The other development of the past decade that is going to force companies to change how they interact with government is the erosion of policy support for economic openness. This has been reflected in the slowdown in global trade liberalization and it means companies must rethink their approach to cross-border expansion and operating practices.

In 2005, the global economy was operating on overdrive and grew 4.7 percent. It expanded by another 5.3 percent the following year — marking one of the strongest two-year periods of global growth in decades. The robust expansion reflected, in part, the commitment governments throughout the world had made to deeper economic integration and more open markets. Trade and investment barriers had been falling, and in November 2001 the members of the World Trade Organization (who represented the overwhelming share of global economic output) agreed to move forward with an agenda of comprehensive trade liberalization. The agreement reflected a belief among government leaders throughout much of the world that economic openness would spur growth and long-term strategic advantage.

But the commitment to openness withered in the wake of the economic slowdown brought on by the 2008 financial crisis. The use of tariff trade barriers applied to products imported by G20 economies (which account for 85 percent of global GDP) rose 33 percent from 2007-2013, according to the World Bank.[3] And in the years that followed, some of the standout emerging economies retreated to old habits. Russia's seizure of parts of Ukraine in 2014 highlighted the backsliding. Brazil, which achieved 7.6 percent economic growth in 2010, has dramatically slowed (its growth rate in 2014 was just 0.1 percent). More broadly, a commodity boom attracted countries' focus and many also became less economically fixated on the convergence of physical and digital assets. This was accompanied by a retreat to a pre-information age posture focused on imposing trade and investment restrictions or simply refusing to open up their markets further.

Adding to the dilemma, WTO members failed to close on the agreed agenda negotiated in 2001. Many countries, such as China and India, who had fared quite well under existing WTO trade regimes, saw little upside in resetting the rules, while many G-7 countries came to the negotiating table in a halfhearted way. Amid the trade stalemate, the WTO's ability to serve as an effective motivator for openness and integration calcified, and momentum for economic integration stalled.

No major country has yet asserted itself as an impactful global leader in support of a new worldwide trading regime, and many governments are viewing new areas of potential growth (such as digital business models and big data analytics) as being as much of a threat as an opportunity. Hence, the status quo is a more comfortable and less risky path to keep.

The leadership that is being exercised is at the regional level. The launch of initiatives such as the Trans-Pacific Partnership, the Trans-Atlantic Trade and Investment Partnership, and the African Union's Continental Free Trade Area (CFTA) demonstrate there is still interest among some countries in opening markets. The difficulty of making those initiatives succeed, and how much worldwide liberalization is sacrificed during the negotiating process, will be an indicator of just how much political support there is for greater openness.

The pervasiveness of the digital domain and the expansion of transparency, coupled with the slowdown in trade liberalization, has forced companies to rethink their approach to a wide range of issues. For example, how vulnerable is a supply chain (physical or digital) when cybersecurity attacks can come from any part of the world without warning? What impact does this have on one's brand? What is the best market access approach to select when governments in emerging economies have greater demand-side influence? And what will be the impact over one's intellectual property or foreign exchange needs?

For business leaders, the last ten years have brought foundational changes to their operating environment. Looking ahead, governments throughout the world will continue to be buffeted by digital issues and trade tensions. They will make decisions involving these and other factors that will strike at the heart of how companies will operate. As former U.S. Senator Joe Lieberman once remarked to me, "History gives us no rest."

The decade ahead

The decade ahead is destined to bring even more sweeping change to governments. Three changes in particular will be noteworthy in the context of implications for companies. The first will be the aging of populations. The second will be a gradual reshuffling of countries' economic influence on the global stage. And the third will be the emergence of what's known as the "demand-side economy," in which consumers can increasingly dictate what products and services they want, and when they will buy them, as opposed to simply accepting what is supplied to them. These developments will help shape the perception of individual countries and their governments which will, in turn, influence how and where companies invest their resources.

These and other factors will be influenced by the technology-driven trend toward even greater data and information storage, retrieval, and transparency. The continued proliferation of products, from video-enabled smart phones to community surveillance cameras to bio-metric identifiers to wearable technology to voice-activated transmission of information, will test governments and not only their ability to perform their stated roles but how they are viewed and held accountable by others.

Demographics

Prior to the 1970s, one of the obstacles to economic growth in many countries was a large population, which needed to be fed and cared for. But as trade liberalization advanced, information technology and networks provided the tools for economic integration. The Internet and the World Wide Web enfranchised individuals and helped to create more integrated and scalable global markets. A large population, now far from being a handicap, became a competitive advantage — assuming it was complemented by public policy supportive of economic growth.

The decade ahead presents new starting points for many governments. As they strive to advance their economic standing and assets, one of the fundamental challenges that will face governments around the world will be demographics. China, the United States, and European Union countries will see the median age of their populations rise, as the birthrate in China and the EU falls and as America's baby boomers reach retirement age. In China today, there are approximately five income earners for each senior citizen. It's projected that by 2030, the ratio will only be 2.5 to 1. And by 2050, just 1.6 to 1. The rising share of non-working adults will stress governments in at least two ways, as they experience declining tax revenue and increased pension obligations.

But in many emerging economies, the demographic profile is much more favorable. For example, in the Middle East and North Africa, 60 percent of the population is under the age of 25. Asia, Indonesia, the Philippines, Malaysia, and Cambodia are projected by the United Nations to see continued growth in the size of their working-age populations until 2050. The biggest demographic dividend will come from India, which is projected to see its working-age population increase by 125 million over the next decade. With increased spending power, these individuals will be buying everything from cars to household products and generating economic output that will contribute to higher living standards.

How will governments in these younger-trending countries view companies that want to invest and expand? What about governments in older-trending countries? In the "older" countries, the potential for a prolonged slowdown in economic growth may lead governments to try to protect domestic industries by raising tariffs or restricting foreign investments unless they re-evaluate longstanding definitions of "working age" and make policy adjustments to new "working life expectancies." And while the economic outlook tied to demographics is more favorable for the "younger" countries, any number of scenarios — such as political instability, government policies limiting economic engagement with other nations of the world, and weak commitment to contemporary human and physical infrastructure investments — could lead governments to adopt mercantilist policies. Every government in every country will differ, of course, which underscores the importance of companies making long-term commitments to engage with government officials, understand the circumstances shaping local markets, and develop ways to raise brand identity with government officials and earn their trust.

A rebalancing of economic influence

One clear theme for the decade ahead will be a more prominent place on the global stage for developing nations. This will reflect not only the size and strength of their economies but also a determination to have their interests better represented within multilateral organizations and throughout the world. Just as companies are always seeking to achieve greater freedom in how they manage their operations, countries also want more freedom to act in ways that they believe will advance their interests. That process is well underway with emerging markets.

Today, emerging markets account for 50 percent of the global economy — up from 31 percent in 1980. While the economic growth that underpins this progress has been a byproduct of many different factors, a few stand out: openness to trade and integrating with the global economy, a public policy environment that's supportive of innovation and entrepreneurship, political stability, an embrace of market-driven standards, and rising educational achievement. Emerging market countries are also more stable, and much better positioned to absorb the shocks that have frequently destabilized their economies in the past. Consider that central bank foreign-exchange reserves increased from $610 billion in 1999 to $7.5 trillion in June 2015.

China is the most compelling example of an emerging market country that now has more choices about the policies it can pursue, and in turn, use to influence others around the world. China (and other high-growth economies) has been disillusioned with its influence and the pace of reform at multilateral organizations such as the World Bank and IMF. While the country has been designated as the world's largest economy (in terms of purchasing power parity), it holds less than 5 percent of the votes within the World Bank. The United States, by comparison, holds more than 16 percent, and the gulf is even bigger at the International Monetary Fund. Given its economic scale, China's ability to exercise freedom of economic action enhances its influence globally. Its work to launch the Asian Infrastructure Investment Bank (AIIB) in June 2015, with 56 other countries, is an excellent example. It reflects not only a desire but an ability to show independent leadership in helping the region meet its future infrastructure needs.

China is also working to strengthen its position on the global stage by trying to globalize its currency. It is seeking to have the yuan (RMB) designated a reserve currency by the IMF, which will reduce the influence of the U.S. dollar. Consider that 25 percent of the country's international trade was conducted using the yuan in 2014, while just five years earlier, the share had been 0.02 percent.

Another emblem of the rise of emerging market country influence has been the so-called "BRICS" countries (Brazil, Russia, India, China and South Africa). They have created their own development bank and held seven summits to promote their shared interests.

Where might this new economic influence be exercised? In addition to the World Bank, IMF, World Health Organization (WHO), UN, and the World Intellectual Property Organization (WIPO), emerging market countries are members of the G-20 — a multilateral forum for international economic co-operation whose members account for 85 percent of global economic output. Combine this with the growth of other developing countries such as Indonesia, Mexico, and Turkey, and you have a very different landscape for business managers to operate in — more diverse and less tied to a western economic market model.

While the interests of emerging market countries are far from monolithic, these countries are increasingly banding together to help ensure that certain baseline priorities are protected within multilateral organizations and when the rules of trade are being written. This speaks to the need for companies operating across borders to deepen their engagement with governments in emerging markets and to embrace operating structures — such as those embodied in the globally integrated enterprise — that deepen their presence in these countries.

G-20 trending assessment

From a management standpoint, any company choosing to operate in a market would analyze the forces shaping that market. While the G-20 has many detractors, it nevertheless represents governments coming together on a regular basis to set economic direction for 85 percent of global GDP. Accordingly, it is worthy of some reflection, with a focus on how its dynamics can inform business decision-making for firms operating globally.

Again, if governments can make, modify, and eliminate markets overnight, it's instructive to consider how countries' economic fortitude and influence has changed and may indeed shape the future of the global economy. The following G-20 competitiveness rankings (as determined by the World Economic Forum) have changed over the past decade.[4] The table to the right ranks the G-20 countries using 12 criteria, which include the quality of a country's institutions, its infrastructure, and the macroeconomic environment.[5] Drawing on the WEF criteria and over 35 years of my own experiences with governments, I have created an extension of the table to forecast how I think countries will trend between now and 2020.

G20 countries ranked for competitiveness

G-20 Countries Rankings

Competitiveness 2005	Competitiveness 2015	Projected Influence 2020
1. United States	1. United States	1. United States
2. Germany	2. Germany	2. China
3. United Kingdom	3. Japan	3. India
4. Japan	4. United Kingdom	4. Germany
5. France	5. Canada	5. Japan
6. Canada	6. Australia	6. South Korea
7. Australia	7. France	7. United Kingdom
8. South Korea	8. Saudi Arabia	8. Australia
9. Saudi Arabia*	9. South Korea	9. Canada
10. Italy	10. China	10. Mexico
11. South Africa	11. Indonesia	11. South Africa
12. India	12. Turkey	12. Indonesia
13. China	13. Italy	13. France
14. Russia	14. Russia	14. Turkey
15. Argentina	15. South Africa	15. Brazil
16. Brazil	16. Brazil	16. Saudi Arabia
17. Mexico	17. Mexico	17. Russia
18. Indonesia	18. India	18. Italy
19. Turkey	19. Argentina	19. Argentina

*Not ranked until 2007

Indonesia and Turkey achieved the biggest gains from 2005-2015, moving up seven positions, while the biggest declines were recorded by India (down six spots) and Argentina (down four spots).

But as we have said earlier, many factors determine the success of governments to advance their standing in the world politically and economically. The third column in the table above offers my assessment of the trending economic influence of G-20 members over the next five years. In addition to considering their size, growth rates, and active economic engagement with the world, I considered government and political stability, economic flexibility, fiscal health and discipline, and willingness to constructively collaborate with other nations to solve problems. I expect China and India to assert themselves and challenge the influence of the United States in shaping the character of the global economy.

In looking at this list, and the ability of governments to shape markets not only within their own borders but also around the world, companies and their management should ask the following: How are we preparing ourselves for the opportunities — or challenges — that will accompany the rebalancing of economic influence among the governments of countries comprising 85 percent of the world's GDP?

Demand-side economy

Another significant development in the context of governments and companies is the emergence of the demand-side economy. Whether you think of this as the rise of the platform economy, the emergence of a sharing economy, or just the ability of individuals to "go direct," economic investments are increasingly being organized by the power of the purchaser. This has significant impact on how governments have made their own choices as rule makers, investors, and purchasers.

For centuries, consumers have primarily had to settle for the products that companies chose for the marketplace. Consumers rarely had the ability to get the unique product they wanted. This was the supply-side economy. Today, due to the realities of technological mobility, connectivity, and computing, consumers have a much greater ability to dictate the precise products they will buy. They can customize virtually anything and, even more important, with the advent of 3-D printing, they can create their own products at the volume and scale they need. To reflect this shift, consider the motto of a new and successful 3-D printing company: "Shapeways Enables Everyone to Bring Their Ideas to Life." Note how that differs from the historic motto of the iconic and highly successful enterprise GE: "We Bring Good Things to Life."

Governments will need to come to grips with this shift in the economic contract between buyers and sellers, as the new arrangements are likely to influence how companies make decisions about where to invest in operations. Governments in developing countries in particular will need to understand this changing dynamic. If low-cost manufacturing can be carried out at roughly the same price in developed countries, then much of the rationale for locating in developing countries disappears. That could have profound consequences for foreign direct investment flows not only to these developing countries but also to developed countries with, perhaps, aging populations.

A new day has dawned and the interactions between companies and governments will be impacted in meaningful ways.

The power and impact of transparency

In her earlier chapter, Shelly Lazarus explained that in the age of transparency and instant communication, companies must ensure their brand is consistent throughout the world. Governments face a similar challenge. Their brand will become better known globally, and they will face criticism and suspicion if their actions don't align with their rhetoric.

Heightened transparency will increase the importance for companies with cross-border operations to develop a full understanding of the brand attached to their home country government. Today the situation facing the foreign affiliates of U.S.-based companies is particularly acute. Those affiliates working in sensitive sectors, such as technology, will face suspicion that they are working in tandem with the U.S. government — a suspicion fed by the disclosure that following the 2001 terrorist attacks American telephone companies provided domestic calling records to the National Security Agency. These companies could find themselves severely handicapped as they pursue new opportunities, particularly involving government contracts.

Consider the case of Brazil. Its president, Dilma Rousseff, condemned the NSA after learning that the agency had intercepted some of her communications. So it was not entirely surprising that Brazil announced in November 2014 that it would not allow U.S. vendors to bid on a $185 million contract to build an undersea fiber-optic cable to Portugal. The head of Telebras, the state-owned telecom company overseeing the project, cited concerns about "data integrity and vulnerability."

This is far from an isolated example. In 2013, the Information Technology & Innovation Foundation (ITIF) estimated that U.S. companies could forgo up to $35 billion in revenue through 2016, reflecting concerns that these companies could be vulnerable to U.S. government pressure to share sensitive information. Two years later, ITIF said the economic impact of the surveillance practices will likely "far exceed" the earlier estimate, observing that "foreign customers are shunning U.S. companies."[6] Among the many examples cited was the German government blocking Verizon from providing Internet service to government departments, citing the potential for the NSA to get access to Verizon's network and spy on German government officials.

It's not only companies headquartered in the United States that face these suspicions. In one celebrated case, a company based in the United Arab Emirates, Dubai Ports World, was ensnared in controversy in 2006 after it was approved to manage six U.S. seaports. Critics in the U.S. Congress and elsewhere charged that because the company was owned by the government in the UAE, it could leave the ports vulnerable to terrorist acts, even though the UAE was one of America's strongest allies in the Middle East. Under pressure, the company sold its U.S. operations to a company headquartered in the United States.

While skirmishes like these make headlines, there are countless other episodes in which companies are interacting with government officials on matters large and small. Whether these interactions prove successful is frequently dictated by whether individual companies have invested the time and resources needed to effectively engage with the governments in these countries. That engagement can deepen understanding of the economic and business expertise companies bring to the relationship and how it contributes to the national agenda and goals of a nation.

Engaging government and building trust

During my 25 years with IBM, I received regular reminders of the importance attached to engaging with the governments of nations (and even small communities) where we were investing and operating. We believed that if IBM was going to grow, governments needed to at least respect us and be neutral toward us. Preferably, they would be impressed with our capabilities and would help enable our mutual success. Therefore, our approach to governmental affairs was to constantly bring future-shaping value to a government and to do so in highly ethical and accountable ways — accountable to IBM internal stakeholders, external shareholders, and collaborators.

Our engagement took many different forms but always was grounded in annual goals and objectives relevant to IBM's growth. Sometimes it was as predictable as weighing in during the consideration of a government policy. Other times it included co-investing with government to build better schools, expand and train human talent for employment in the high tech sector, build R&D facilities and cutting-edge technology breakthroughs, use IT to improve public sector operations, or help develop a more modern and innovative infrastructure. Our objective was to become more than just another multinational company; instead, we wanted to become a trusted partner that could deliver insights and long-term value from around the world to countries and their citizens. We understood that trust would be the most powerful — and enduring — currency of all and that earning trust is more important than buying praise.

I regularly joined with IBM's former CEO and my colleague, Samuel Palmisano, to present our company's bona fides and commitment to the highest levels of government. Sam explained his thinking about engaging with governments in his 2014 book, *Re-Think: A Path to the Future*:

[H]elping a region — or entire country — to advance its standard of living (particularly through education) will help earn the trust of government officials and make it much easier to achieve market access. And make no mistake — this trust must be earned, and that can only happen through behavior and actions, not through marketing. While at IBM I characterized this as getting "permission to operate," and over time we saw that our identity as an "American" company mattered less than the indigenous value we created in the countries where we were doing business.

The value creation started with generating jobs, making local investments, paying taxes and bringing high-quality, trustworthy products and services to new buyers. But it went beyond that. We saw that we could create more value — for the society and for IBM — by doing more than entering a market. As I have argued here, *making* a market involves working with leaders in business, government, academia and community organizations to help advance their national agenda and address their societal needs — whether those needs involve better schools, more robust public safety, more modern infrastructure, or something else altogether. In short, we would strive to build real skills in the local workforce and enable new capabilities among the citizenry. We consciously worked to serve as a force for modernization and progress.

Despite the power governments have to create and shape markets, some company leaders will ask more narrowly whether it's worth the time and money to develop a functional expertise and infrastructure focused on relations with government (both domestic and foreign). Is there a top or bottom line benefit that can come from approaching my business this way? Is it really core to my business? The answer is yes.

I have seen many examples of high-growth companies based in the United States (often in the technology sector) and elsewhere that are slow to realize the importance of engaging government in a holistic manner. They take a dismissive attitude toward the creaky machinery of government and essentially declare, "…just leave us alone." Or many companies think everything will be ok by just making calls on key government officials. This will surely build a trusting relationship…right?! Both come up short if one is serious about being allowed to operate your business with flexibility and to help shape the future.

For companies operating globally, it can be tempting to ignore public policy altogether, since engagement requires interacting with multiple governments when that time and energy could be devoted to other business functions. But this is rarely a successful or sustainable strategy, particularly as the companies continue to grow. Microsoft engaged little with the U.S. government until facing an anti-trust trial in the late 1990s. Google took a hands-off approach to global government relations and today faces an anti-trust investigation in Europe. Uber, by contrast, has been more aggressive in its efforts to engage with state and local officials throughout the world — a move taken by necessity, given the impassioned resistance of cities and non-Uber drivers feeling threatened by its existence.

One episode from my time at IBM speaks to the value of engagement. My team led, with colleagues in Japan and the IBM tax department, an effort to get the United States and Japan to sign a tax treaty that would eliminate a number of economic inefficiencies, such as withholding of taxes on royalties and dividends. Removing these inefficiencies would bring liquidity back to each country's economy and potentially increase investment flows. We helped create and lead a bilateral coalition, formed in 2001, that included a number of other large American companies operating in Japan, as well as Japanese companies operating in the U.S. We worked through associations such as the National Foreign Trade Council and the U.S.-Japan Business Council. Our advocacy proved effective, and the U.S. and Japan eventually signed the treaty, which took effect in January 2005. The dividend paid by our engagement was quite significant, as the treaty added 6 cents per share/year (or roughly $145 million USD) to IBM's bottom line.

Or consider a different example from Tata, the India-based conglomerate that operates in multiple industries (including cars — it owns Jaguar Land Rover) and multiple countries. In 2012, three Tata companies were ranked in the top six of *Fortune India's* Most Admired Firms. Tata took a methodical approach to building trust with local governments, as described by David Beier, Ed Freeman, Dean Krehmeyer, and Chris Williams in a 2015 paper for the Center for Global Enterprise:

> Tata's reputation isn't an accident. Tata companies have earned it through a deep commitment to the wellbeing of the communities in which they operate, through initiatives ranging from providing housing to steel workers to securing fresh water for local villages. These initiatives aren't isolated outreach, and they go beyond simply donating funds to good causes. Rather, reputation and trust is maintained in a very careful, proactive way through the use of an advanced stakeholder mapping strategy.

> The Tata Nano — the world's first $1,000 car (the price has since risen to about $2,400) — is perhaps the achievement for which Tata is most known outside of India. The Nano was originally intended to be built in West Bengal. However, in 2008 local farmers groups were agitated by government land seizures around the factory, and as the situation grew dire Tata Motors' management announced that they would seek a new home for the Nano.

> Such a decision might have meant years of delays, but Tata Motors didn't have to wait even a week. The very same day it announced the closure of the West Bengal factory, Tata Motors received no less than five invitations from Indian state governments, asking them to relocate to their jurisdictions. Famously, Gujarat State Minister Narendra Modi sent Tata Group chief Ratan Tata an SMS — 'Welcome to Gujarat'. Within three days, Gujarat state procured land for Tata outside of Ahmedabad. Tata Motors' new factory was producing Nanos in just 14 months.

Tata Motors reputation made it possible for the Guajarati government to facilitate private sector goals. Moreover, the speed at which the firm was able to overcome a difficult nonmarket challenge is indicative of the value that the Indian government placed on Tata's reputation. In this instance, Tata Motors' diligent stakeholder mapping strategy, designed to build reputation and trust throughout Tata's entire ecosystem, has paid great dividends.

While few companies are as large as Tata, the lesson nonetheless applies to companies operating anywhere — and particularly outside their home market. As the authors point out, "The most concrete benefit of building trust with governments, and those who align with them, is the opportunity to open new markets. Governments are important customers, and, as with any customer, need to trust the firms that are selling products or services to them. The same key components to securing trust (e.g. transparency, honesty, consistency, respect and commitment to the larger community) are qualities governments are looking for in suppliers or business partners."

Optimizing a management model for global success

The core value of government affairs is two-fold. Done right, it brings expertise about government and its three roles into the company to sharpen business decision-making and execution in order to create external growth accelerators and avoid growth barriers. It also helps communicate (some would say translate) to government officials the expertise of the company and how government can rely on it to achieve its economic and societal objectives.

In today's environment the ability to construct a government affairs function that collects multi-cultural expertise and builds a truly global team is easier than ever before. Information tools and data-gathering capabilities have made the activity of global government affairs more manageable and immediate. For CEOs and other senior leaders, the key management factor is to ground the function's capability in public policy expertise relevant to the company's current and future business, and to government's agenda. Strategy and policy objectives should be developed globally but they must draw upon local knowledge and insights, because execution is local and will remain so as long as governments exist.

Regardless of what government affairs organizational model a company chooses to deploy, there are six guidelines that should ground their efforts:

1. Ensure objectives are globally consistent and locally relevant, because in the age of transparency any inconsistencies are destined to be uncovered and disseminated.

2. Understand that in relationships with government officials, the "what" (the product, service, or expertise companies are offering), is much more important than the "who" (the identities of those managing the relationships within the company and within the government). Making a difference is more important than making a statement.

3. Be able to articulate your added value. Set your agenda focused on what is needed from society and government. What knowledge, service, or product do you offer that distinguishes you from the competition and how does it benefit society and government? If policymakers can see your company is contributing to progress in their communities, this will lay the groundwork for a sustainable and trusted working relationship.

4. Build a skill profile for government affairs personnel that is based on a culture of accountability — for external results brought into the company and internal competencies brought out to government. Clear and annual objectives should be especially communicated to internal stakeholders.

5. Understand that in the eyes of the government you are one brand — regardless of whether you are a publicly-traded company, a privately-held corporation, a state-owned enterprise,

or a family business. To the outside world, governance divisions don't matter. Don't take solace in company-constructed silos. You are one enterprise and, hence, one reputation.

6. Develop a leadership team that is keen to understand and appreciate government, and that wants to actively shape the future even when it may not be comfortable to do so. Remember, growth and comfort don't co-exist. This can be a critical source of competitive advantage for your company.

Conclusion

In today's world, the pace of change — encompassing technology, business models, and potential markets in which to do business — seems to be accelerating at speeds that make it difficult to keep up. Businesses strive to assess the impact of this "environment of velocity" on their operating and financial models. Governments face even greater challenges to understand and adjust to rapid changes that are induced by technology and transparency. Both entities need each other to constructively navigate through the uncertainty of the future, especially if they are to advance the human condition while doing so.

The interdependence of business and government is a reality. The constructive character of the relationship will be determined by the wisdom and behavior of each party. It is incumbent on global business leaders to realize they have both an obligation and an opportunity to help governments and society shape a brighter tomorrow. Governments have a similar responsibility to allow business leaders the ability to create that tomorrow in an efficient and flexible way.

Those enterprises that engage government — this market force like no other — in value-added ways, and develop trusted relationships, will discover that they have greater freedom to operate and are better equipped to realize long-term growth and success.

Spurring Creative Genius for Society's Benefit

David J. Kappos

Centuries of history have proven that the surest way to encourage investment in innovation is the promise of a meaningful return on that investment when an innovation is successful. And that promise is fulfilled by Intellectual Property Rights (IPR). Patent, trademark, trade secret and copyright laws tell firms of all sizes — and indeed humanity generally — that innovation will be rewarded by offering an attractive bargain between innovators and society. While the first intellectual property protection is thought to have been granted in ancient Greece about 2,500 years ago (the equivalent of one-year patents were issued to chefs for select recipes), IP began to take on heightened importance in countries such as the United States as inventors came forward with transformative new products and had them patented. These products included the cotton gin (patented in 1794), the telephone (1876), and the airplane (1906).

Today, IP is considered an essential component of advanced and growing societies. Thus, it's easy to overlook that every aspect of modern life is the product of innovations rooted in intellectual property, from smart phones to hybrid cars to life-saving medical treatments, many of which would have been unimaginable 100, 50, or even 20 years ago. More broadly, IP is a source of wealth and job creation. In the United States, IP-intensive industries accounted for 34 percent the country's gross domestic product (GDP) in 2010, and 27 percent of all jobs. In European Union countries, IP-intensive industries accounted for 39 percent of GDP during the years 2008-13 and 26 percent of all jobs. And those numbers will only grow larger with time.

A decade of change

Given the critical role IP plays in modern economies, it's useful to understand the ways in which the IP climate has evolved over the past decade.

First, as the world community has moved through the various economic ages — agriculture, industrial, information — IP has taken on a more important role in the global economy. In an economy increasingly driven by knowledge and information, ideas matter more and need more robust protection. It's also the case that the traditional sources of competitive advantage (e.g., commodities and labor, first-mover advantage, access to finance, advanced manufacturing techniques) have dissipated as potential competitors around the world increasingly have access to the same resources. With few or no other sources of competitive advantage available in the modern era, companies can achieve a competitive advantage either through legitimate means (such as developing a breakthrough product) or illegitimate ones (such as counterfeiting). This struggle can be summed up as "first movers vs. fast followers." As a result, IP laws have become the best way — and sometimes the only way — to protect innovation and fairly reward those members of society keen to improve the human condition through new approaches.

This increased emphasis on IP is not a north/south trend, or a developed/developing economy trend — it is a global trend. Chinese companies, for example, cite theft of IP by other Chinese companies as one of their top issues. Patent filings are increasing worldwide, including in Europe, Asia, and America. Those filings indicate that innovators increasingly view patents as an essential tool to protect their competitive advantage.

Second, there has been a greater prevalence of IP abuse over the past decade, particularly related to patents, and these abuses have attracted more attention. The abuses are largely carried out by so-called "patent trolls" — individuals or companies that acquire patent rights merely to file lawsuits claiming patent infringement. While many of the claims go nowhere, and many of the lawsuits that get filed are dismissed, the legal wrangling still brings a significant cost — many millions of dollars per year in lawyer fees and lost productivity.

Third, there's been a backlash against the patent system generally, which has created the most hostile environment toward IP in the United States that I've seen during my 25+ year legal career. The hostility is found in the media, but also all three branches of the U.S. government. The Supreme Court heard more patent cases in 2014 than in any other year in U.S. history, and its decisions overwhelmingly curtailed IP rights. Also in 2014, members of Congress introduced more than a dozen bills related to IP, and most of them were meant to diminish the strength of the patent system in various ways. And the Obama Administration has called for cutbacks in the IP system, while also overruling a landmark IP-related order by the U.S. International Trade Commission — the first such veto in more than three decades.

Lastly, over the past decade, more and more content is being stored and distributed directly via the Internet using smart phones, tablet computers and cloud computing services. This has ushered in new benefits for the sharing of creative works and ideas, along with new challenges to the rights of content creators. As more content gets stored in the cloud and distributed directly to an individual's devices either by command or automatically, new IP challenges arise regarding copyright protection in the era of the Internet of Things.

IP conflict and confusion

One recent dispute is emblematic of how IP issues are being thrust into new terrain and facing heightened scrutiny. The mapping of the human genome has unlocked extraordinary new levels of understanding about the human body and how to treat disease. Approximately 4,000 genes — about 20 percent of the genome — are covered by patents, which have been awarded to entities that discovered a gene or a sequence of DNA. For patented genes, licenses are needed by anyone conducting an experiment that involves these genes.

In 2009, two of those patents — for genes associated with breast cancer (BRCA1 and BRCA2) — were challenged by a collection of plaintiffs who argued that private companies should not be permitted to patent gene sequences. While genetics cases account for a small share of IP cases, the fundamental issues were the same as those pervading the current anti-patent environment: how to reward innovation (the patent holder in this case had pinpointed the location and sequence of both genes) while providing the public with access to the fruits of that innovation at a reasonable cost. In 2013, the U.S. Supreme Court ruled unanimously that isolated human genes could not be patented (though it also ruled that synthetic DNA could be patented). Then in a similar case brought in Australia, that country's highest court reached the opposite conclusion, based on what experts have viewed as policy and science at least as valid as that relied on by the U.S. Supreme Court. Regardless of whether one agrees or disagrees with the U.S. Supreme Court's decision, the case is a reminder of how IP can play a pivotal role in a wide range of debates, and how challenging it is to balance an incentive system aimed at spurring long-term, high risk technology investments (the patent system) with the natural inclination of the public to want today's successful technology solutions at the lowest possible cost.

The BRCA case is also a reminder that when "intellectual property" is in the news, the story is often about conflict: lawsuits between corporate giants fighting over smart phone designs, pirates distributing illicit copies of bestselling movies and music, and foreign hackers attempting to steal innovative companies' valuable engineering know-how. Much of the conflict, while unfortunate, is a byproduct of something positive: societies that are highly dynamic and innovative. That dynamism and innovation inevitably unleashes efforts to appropriate technical breakthroughs, which in turn triggers litigation focused on protecting and enforcing IP rights. While IP-driven conflict would be greatly curtailed in a society with no innovation, such a society would inevitably confront many more serious problems than legal wrangling.

Media coverage of IP conflicts can leave the impression that the IP system is an impediment to innovation, benefiting patent holders to the detriment of the public. The reality is just the opposite. The system, and patents in particular, embody the timeless wisdom of Sir Isaac Newton: "If I have seen further it is only by standing on the shoulders of giants."

Newton was implicitly speaking to the compact that exists between a society and its inventors who are granted patents: the inventions are publicly disclosed so that any skilled person can understand and recreate them. Inventors cannot keep their inventions secret but must contribute their knowledge to the public. And while others are prevented from copying a patented invention for the term of the patent (as part of the bargain to the inventors), interested parties can learn from the published patent description and improve on the invention of others. In this manner, the IP system creates an ever-growing repository of knowledge for the benefit of humankind. That knowledge builds on the innovative ideas of others — ideas that can come from almost anywhere. Similarly, businesses based on those ideas can come from anywhere. Countless companies — if not entire industries — are the byproduct of creating consumer demand for a product, such as the touch-screen tablet computer, where none existed previously.

The decade ahead

When information and content are always available and transparent, innovators must be prepared to play offense *and* defense with their IP assets. That means seeking patents for innovations and ensuring these patents are enforced — in a climate marked by widespread infringement. As such, I expect IP disputes will continue to play a prominent — and pivotal — role across the world's economic and legal landscape during the next 10 years. Indeed, the stresses on the IP system will likely escalate, for a simple reason: technology is going to make it progressively easier to share and copy products, and laws preventing new forms of copying (like all laws) lag behind technological progress.

Looking ahead, I see six overarching "megatrends" — areas where a number of important patterns of activity are converging — that will have significant impact on the creative economy of the future.

The first megatrend is found in the changing means of access and consumption. Location and access are becoming increasingly decoupled — a particular song, for example, once downloaded to a single consumer's home server can be streamed to her office, to her car or to her mobile device while thousands of miles away — and intermediaries that were once part of the physical distribution chain from creator to consumer are playing a less obtrusive but invaluable (and more complex) role in the process. The shift in distribution models toward instantaneous and ubiquitous access are probable sources of friction, with delivery frameworks that cannot or do not embrace the full extent of capabilities offered by modern networks and mobile devices.

The second megatrend is a predictable one: new technologies. Big data, increasingly complex virtual content, 3D printing and technology convergence will be key drivers in how products and services are created and disseminated. These technological advances will lead to increases in efficiency, while also enhancing the creative process itself. And as technologies like 3D printing proliferate, there will be a lively debate (which will likely end up in the courts) as to whether there are sufficient incentives to pursue innovation in an era where replication is so easy. When will replication be legal and when will it be infringement?

The third megatrend is seen in increased user involvement. The creative process is more than ever a shared endeavor, a reality perhaps best exemplified by the 100,000 active contributors to the popular online resource Wikipedia. A range of new licensing choices provides a wealth of options from which user-contributors can tailor access to their IP. The potential blurring of traditional lines between content creators and users raises serious challenges with respect to ownership and rights to the resulting content.

The fourth megatrend lies at the convergence of shifting business models. Traditional business models will see increased pressure from new business models that rely on distributors' lower marginal costs of production and consumers' shift in preference away from ownership in favor of obtaining licenses to access the products they desire. A salient example of the impact of shifting business models is offered by the music industry. A combination of piracy and business model disruption reduced annual global music industry revenues from $30 billion in 1999 to $16.5 billion in 2012. And yet, as subscription services have rapidly expanded, 2012 brought the first year-over-year growth in the music industry since 1999, providing an indication that new models of distribution can meet consumer expectations while at the same time protecting the interests of content owners.

The fifth megatrend focuses on the increasingly global market for products and services. Globalized commerce, when properly leveraged, is a win-win for consumers and providers. Consumers will see a wider range of choices while providers will have access to larger and larger audiences — especially considering the growth of the middle class in emerging economies. Yet globalization also will test the limits of IP legal frameworks which are nationally oriented and were developed before the spread of high-speed global networks. Existing international agreements serve an important role but are unlikely to suffice as the creative and innovative economy increasingly comes to depend on cross-border licensing.

The sixth and final megatrend that has a critical bearing on IP development is the increased fragmentation of IP ownership. More than ever, thanks to the Internet and collaborative innovation between multiple parties, joint and derivative works are playing a central role in product and content creation, as existing works are increasingly adapted, excerpted, repurposed and incorporated into new works. Ensuring that the rights of original innovators and creators are respected will be essential in the context of this expanding "collaborate and remix" culture. The longstanding problem posed by licensing transaction costs and orphan works (works for which the copyright owner is unknown or unreachable) will become even more challenging in this context, and IP authorities worldwide can be expected to develop new solutions to address this exigency.

So what does all this mean at the country level, and how will IP owners manage through these changing times? I expect many countries in Europe and Asia to strengthen their IP systems. There is a growing awareness in these countries of the nexus between innovation and economic growth. And at a time when growth is slowing in many countries, there is renewed interest in fostering innovation. This sentiment will be even more pronounced in countries that have large numbers of highly educated scientists and engineers, such as India and China. While IP violations have been widespread in both countries for years, I think domestic industry in both countries is going to place renewed pressure on their respective governments to enact more robust IP laws and tighten enforcement so as to ensure their own newly created IP is protected.

Given market trends and developments this pressure is likely to come from the pharmaceutical and life sciences industries in particular. The traditional approach of relying on U.S. companies to pursue drug discovery, and then finding ways to access those new drugs (legally or illegally), will be insufficient. Health care-focused companies in both countries will see the demand for drugs that cater to a domestic clientele and will want protections for those drugs once they are developed. Given the size of the Chinese and Indian economies, their support for more robust protections will be a very positive development for the global IP regime, and more importantly for patients seeking treatment in those countries and elsewhere.

Building a better — and more global — IPR mousetrap

One of the under-appreciated realities of intellectual property is that while it's a key ingredient in the global economy, the legal regime supporting it is decidedly non-global. There has been some movement recently toward greater global collaboration, but intellectual property issues still tend to be addressed country-by-country. More and more we find ourselves struggling along with a "multinational" approach that needs to be rethought in the globally integrated era.

Consider research and development. Over the last generation, it has become truly global. Scientists in London are collaborating in the course of a single business day with counterparts in Guanzhou, Bangalore, Stuttgart, Sao Paulo, and Sunnyvale. Together, these scientists generate brilliant new ideas that lead to wonderful new products and services and, of course, patent filings — in at least some of the countries in which collaboration is taking place and frequently in many other countries. But that is where the neat modern system of globally integrated R&D ceases to be neat, modern or global. At this intersection of patent law and cross-border collaboration on research and development, there is a conundrum: where to file an initial patent application for an invention derived from multinational resources?

The root of the problem lies in the nation-based regulatory environment of patent law (*see table on page 75*), with the laws of multiple countries each requiring the filing of affected patent applications first in that country. Protective patent filing laws are easy enough to comply with when only one jurisdiction is implicated. But in the case of inventions developed in various places or by various inventors working together, these protective provisions can quickly come into direct conflict with one another. Indeed, these competing provisions can make filing a patent application in any country a violation of at least one other country's laws.

While the patent regime is a long way from being truly global, there are some important signs of progress. In 2006, the intellectual property offices of the United States and Japan launched a joint program designed to bring greater speed and efficiency to the process of getting patent applications from one country examined in the other. Under the program, which now includes 17 countries, intellectual property offices share information, with the objective of accelerating patent approval times while simultaneously improving quality. Known as the Patent Prosecution Highway, the program has proven very popular with patent applicants, experiencing triple digit growth multiple years running, and savings for patent applicants and patent offices valued in the hundreds of millions of dollars. Some of the countries participating in the effort also belong to a patent work-sharing program known as ASPEC that includes nine nations in ASEAN (the Association of South East Asian Nations). The goal is the same: for patent applicants from participating countries to obtain patents faster and more efficiently, by making it possible to share search and examination results between participating IP offices.

The current patchwork of multinational patent coordination leaves much to be desired. A system that more accurately reflects the global nature of the way business operates would lower patent processing costs for governments while improving economies of scale for innovators. This chart shows the current levels of patent cooperation among 85% of the world's economy as represented by the G-20 (and Singapore).

Country	PCT	CPCS	Global PPH	PPH 2.0	Outsource Search & Examination
Argentina					
Australia	✔		✔	✔	
Brazil	✔				
Canada	✔		✔	✔	
China	✔	Partial	✔		
EU	✔	✔	✔	✔	
France	✔	✔ (via EPO)	✔ (via EPO)	✔ (via EPO)	
Germany	✔	✔ (via EPO)	✔ (via EPO)	✔ (via EPO)	
India	✔				
Indonesia	✔				
Italy	✔	✔ (via EPO)	✔ (via EPO)	✔ (via EPO)	
Japan	✔		✔	✔	
Mexico	✔				
Russia	✔	Partial	✔	✔	
Saudi Arabia					
Singapore	✔		✔	✔	To Australia
South Africa	✔	✔			
South Korea	✔	Partial	✔	✔	
Turkey	✔	✔ (via EPO)	✔ (via EPO)	✔ (via EPO)	
UK	✔	✔	✔	✔	
US	✔	✔	✔	✔	

PCT – Patent Cooperation Treaty   CPCS – Cooperative Patent Classification
PPH – Patent Prosecution Highway   EPO – European Patent Office

The U.S. and the European Union have also made important progress on bringing greater efficiency to the patent system. For more than a century, patent offices throughout the world have used different methods to classify and sort patents (roughly akin to the Dewey Decimal system used in American libraries). When I was director of the U.S. Patent and Trademark Office, we began working with the European patent authorities to harmonize our systems and migrate toward a common classification scheme. That harmonization process is now complete, and the Cooperative Patent Classification (CPC) system has greatly simplified — and accelerated — the patent search process, again while improving quality by ensuring all applicable international prior art is found through a single classification search. It represents an important step toward global IPR recognition and integration.

This emerging shift toward a more cooperative cross-border approach to patent reviews and approvals is akin to the technology sector's decades-long evolution from proprietary standards to open standards. In both instances, there's a focus on building from a shared foundation of knowledge — and not duplicating the work of others. This will be of great value to the IP system, which as I noted earlier is non-global in its operations, with patent offices throughout the world typically repeating the work of their counterparts in other countries before issuing new patents. It is highly inefficient — for both patent applicants and the offices reviewing their applications.

A shared system, with what operationally amounts to "open standards," will lead to higher-quality patents (since patent examiners will be building on the information collected, and the work conducted, in other countries) issued with greater efficiency and at lower cost for both applicants and patent offices. Just as the open standards of the Internet have made it possible for virtually any company to integrate seamlessly into the Internet and Web infrastructures, more open standards for patents can help foster the spread of technology to more places around the world.

Why shouldn't we have an IPR system, with the appropriate safeguards, that reflects the way the global economy operates and creates value 24/7?

The leadership challenges ahead

There are four leadership challenges I see coming. Leaders are well served to begin preparing themselves and their enterprises to gauge the impact these challenges will have on business and financial models.

Expanding the focus on IP

IP has simply become too important to leave to the IP lawyers, or any lawyers for that matter. Lawyers live in a world of risk minimization. IP is about value creation and value extraction, not merely risk minimization. The fruit of IP protection — patents, trademarks, copyrights, know-how — is now tradable for value. IP has become an asset class for which deals of all shapes and sizes can be made. It impacts product pricing, product development, marketing and sales, strategy, finance and budget, research and development. Said differently,

IP impacts the entire business. The business leader in an innovation-reliant industry who ignores or fails to understand the place and value of her IP in her business does so at her own considerable peril. Just ask Apple and Samsung, who have spent billions fighting over patents in recent years.

Balancing the short term and the long term

Amid evolutions in the patent regime, there is a fundamental leadership challenge facing publicly-traded companies: making investments in innovation that may take years to pay dividends while also balancing short-term earnings pressures that come from financial analysts who focus on quarterly earnings. These pressures can tempt companies to curtail their R&D investments in order to juice their stock price. The effect can be lethal, leading to misguided corporate strategies and even a bending of accounting standards. As the noted scholar W. Edwards Deming once observed, "People with targets, and jobs dependent on meeting them, will probably meet the targets — even if they have to destroy the enterprise to do it." The incrementalism that is a hallmark of innovation today, with few big-bang breakthroughs, is a byproduct of the short-termism that has infected so many companies. While I'm proud that my former employer, IBM, has been the leading recipient of U.S. patents for 22 consecutive years, and was awarded more than 7,500 patents in 2014 alone (a single-year record for any company), I also know that R&D is not as embedded in the DNA of all public companies. I expect this challenge of maintaining long-term investments while meeting short-term earnings targets is only going to grow.

Time for a truce in the IP arms race?

Set against that leadership challenge is a related one: whether companies should continue with the IP equivalent of a nuclear arms race — filing for more patents every year, and incurring significant expenses, while realizing gains that are often quite modest. There is no simple answer, and it's made more interesting by the emergence of entities such as ipCreate (led by former IBMers Marshall Phelps and John Cronin) that can help a company create IP on-demand, or buy or license IP that's been developed elsewhere. Thus the decision facing leaders: invest in innovation or acquire what's needed only when you need it and when it fits your precise purpose?

The price of IP protection

Another leadership challenge for companies is determining the level of IP protection they will realize in specific countries and whether the expense associated with securing a patent can be justified. Specifically, leaders facing IP decisions must ask themselves, "what do I get and when do I get it?" The answer will be different for every product in every country, of course. But it's clear that in some countries, such as China, there's a high likelihood of having one's product copied, and absolutely no recourse if it doesn't have a Chinese patent. That's what happened a few years ago when an American manufacturer of recreational camper trailers discovered that an exact replica of its product was being sold in China. The company had not filed for a Chinese patent, and later discovered that the copyist of its camper trailer had patented the product in China.

Conclusion

The patent system is all about expanding the body of knowledge for society's collective benefit. The investments made in the form of temporary exclusive rights have reaped handsome returns for countries around the world — helping breakthrough technologies spread and contribute to a dramatic rise in living standards. While some countries have had more success with innovation than others, in the modern global economy no country or region can be the sole source of the world's new ideas. Continued success in promoting innovation requires international cooperation and a global perspective — one that bridges cultural and legal differences regarding IP systems and encourages innovators around the world to continue investing in innovation.

If the required rethink of the patent regime sparks progress toward a more globally integrated system, I believe countries everywhere will experience a new era of innovation. This "innovation era" can bring forward new transformative products that help overcome many of the world's most pressing challenges, spanning from disease to depletion of the ozone layer, while also unlocking new opportunities to achieve greater growth and prosperity.

Advantage: Supply Chain

Jean-Pascal Tricoire and
Annette Clayton

In tennis, when players reach that point in a game where even play next requires a knock-out process, a score is given called "advantage." Schneider
Electric engages every day in match play around the world with top competitors. We believe that what brings "advantage" to our customers and us is our
supply chain — its scale, agility, efficiency, and responsiveness to the specific
needs of our customers.

We hope in this chapter you will realize, as we have, that taking a decision to
manage such a fundamental part of one's business in an integrated and transparent way is not only the best path to competitive advantage, but an essential
one for the globally integrated economy we find ourselves in today.

Who is Schneider Electric and why Hong Kong?

Our company was founded in 1836, when two brothers, Adolphe and Eugène
Schneider, acquired a collection of mines, foundries, and forges in Le Creu-
sot, a town in eastern France. The company has reinvented itself many times
throughout its long history, with a constant trademark of being at the forefront
of industrial technology changes. Today we are the global specialist in energy
management — providing technology and integrated solutions to optimize

energy use in a number of sectors, including energy and infrastructure, industry, data centers, offices, and residential homes. With more than 180,000 employees spread across offices in more than 100 countries, we generated revenues of €24.9 billion in 2014 — twice as much compared to a decade earlier — and 44 percent of these revenues came from emerging markets. Our core lines of business are residential and non-residential buildings (accounting for 33 percent of our revenue in 2014), industrial and machines (27 percent), utilities and infrastructure (26 percent), and data centers and networks (14 percent).

In view of reflecting our company evolution, we decided in 2011 to move our top management closer to our customers and to local talents by creating three management hubs—Boston, Paris, and Hong Kong. The focus on Asia, in particular, reflected that it was the source for a growing share of our revenue. We also expected the world's economic center of gravity to continue shifting there, given that three of the world's megatrends — urbanization, industrialization, and digitization — were moving with the greatest speed there. And we saw growing demand for energy in Asia. While global demand for electricity is projected to be 76 percent higher in 2030 than it was in 2007, China and India alone will account for more than half of all incremental energy demand. This projected rise will build on the region's robust economic growth rates of the past few decades, which have created a large commercial class and contributed to the growth of Asia-based companies. Today, there are more companies in the Fortune Global 500 from Asia than there are from North America. And China, which is home to 95 of the top 500 companies, has a greater representation than the combined total of companies from France, Germany, and England. The economic growth rates have also created a thriving middle class of consumers, and the number of people in the region's middle class is being projected to increase from about 525 million today to more than 3.2 billion by 2030. That growth is going to create demand for the kind of products, services, and solutions we can provide.

The shift to three management hubs also reinforced our transition from a trans-Atlantic business to a global business. Today, our revenues are almost equally split between the Asia-Pacific (28 percent in 2014), Western Europe (28 percent), North America (25 percent), and the rest of the world (19 percent).

Underpinning our shift to a multipolar management organization and to Asia in particular was a broader recognition that if we — or any other company — were going to emerge in our industry, we would need to do things differently. We couldn't simply follow the path of larger competitors. So we tried to think different and accelerate our transition into a global company. And we did this while preserving our dedication to our customers and our people. Technology has helped us get closer to both, and we are a better — and more competitive — company as a result.

The supply chain as a source of competitive advantage

In the vast majority of manufacturing companies, the supply chain has traditionally been viewed as a cost center — part of the price of doing business but little more than that. We have worked to turn this formula on its head and make our supply chain a source of competitive advantage — for our customers and for us. Fundamental to our strategy has been to embed strategic thinking supply chain leaders into the different lines of business. We believe it helps increase customer satisfaction, and drive topline growth, both of which are fundamental to our long-term competitiveness throughout the world. These leaders ultimately turn the business strategy into the corresponding supply chain requirements for their business without being responsible to operate the supply chain on a day-to-day basis.

The supply chain is fundamental to almost everything we do at Schneider Electric. We fulfill a customer's order every 1.5 seconds, and we have over 200 factories, as well as nearly 100 distribution centers, spread across 44 countries. In short, we have to get the supply chains right if we are going to stay competitive. (We say supply "chains" as there are multiple supply chains required to service our full customer requirements.)

Our supply chains have a big impact on customer satisfaction, because much of our work for customers is focused on delivering and installing mission critical systems. These systems are quite complex and have to be delivered in line with a project timeline as it develops and then be ready to commission the day the system goes live. We find that delivering a tailored experience to every customer creates a true difference. Because for them, time to market has become critical, and if we can help them reduce their time to market, it's a true competitive advantage.

Supply chains at Schneider Electric

We have customers in a wide variety of industries and in countries throughout the world. Given their diverse needs, we are tailoring our supply chain value propositions to different customer buying behaviors. For example, our *collaborative supply chain* involves working to optimize the end-to-end supply chain ecosystem with our customers. It involves co-planning and providing a higher level of visibility between our respective supply chains. And our *lean supply chain* is for customers who are incredibly price sensitive and so we work to control costs at every step of the supply chain. We make supply chain tradeoff decisions that are more sensitive to cost, such as speed of delivery.

Why we organize the way we do

Schneider is organized in accordance with three key concepts: specialization, mutualization and globalization.

Specialization mainly concerns sales and front-office operations. Each country has its own sales force and local leader as soon as it reaches critical mass. It also has a specialized front office in each business line to respond more effectively to customer demand for specific expertise.

Mutualization covers local back-office operations at the country and regional level, with the business organized around operational regions: Global Operations, North America, and China. These regions are split into zones, with empowered Zone Presidents and Country Presidents, which are appointed in each country to oversee all delegated business (and associated income statements), monitor the full transversal P&L of the country, deploy our strategy in the country, and pool local back-office resources.

Globalization concerns the six support functions, known as Global Functions, which are not specific to a given country or business. These functions are finance, marketing, supply chain, human resources, strategy, and information systems.

The transformation of our supply chain

The transformation of our supply chain began in 2011. One of the drivers of the transformation effort was the global financial crisis, which provided a potent reminder of how volatility in one part of the world could infect the entire global economy. The crisis underscored the need for supply chains that could adapt to this volatility. But even more important was our desire to transform the company away from a predominant focus on "product" and toward a focus on projects, solutions, and services offerings. As part of this transformation, we were focused on creating an end-to-end customer-centric approach as well as more differentiated supply chain models.

We launched the "Tailored Supply Chain" program, with the goal of better aligning the supply chain set-up with the needs and behaviors of each customer segment. Six initiatives were defined to support the transformation:

- Develop delivery capabilities differentiated by customer segment

- Build best-in-class planning processes by supply chain model

- Step-up purchasing to drive proactive planning and procurement

- Reduce lead times through optimization of plant and distribution center footprint and logistics network flow design

- Increase partnerships with selected transportation carriers to improve and digitize customer service

- Align the information systems strategy with the supply chain strategy

As we pursued these new models, we re-examined the skills and competencies within our supply chain organization and discovered that we were deficient in many core skills, such as planning, logistics, and purchasing. We also discovered that our supply chain management was fragmented and inconsistently organized. In China, for example, our 30 factories were reporting to many different entities at the level just below the Executive Committee. In addition, 15 factories were not part of our industrial organization, and seven of these were reporting to managers who were not even based in China. This kind of fragmentation existed throughout the world — a byproduct of numerous acquisitions in multiple types of businesses.

A first step in the transformation was to define our overall objectives for simplifying the organization. The objectives we agreed on were to put the customer first, to favor efficiency and productivity, and to foster the interest and the development of our people in the geographies.

Our chief supply chain officer and executive vice president, Annette Clayton, established the design principles of the supply chain. Rather than starting with how people working on supply chain issues should be organized within the company, Annette and her team started by drawing up operating principles, based on customer insights, business issues, country office input, supply chain trends, and long-term challenges we knew we needed to overcome. They worked to answer a number of key questions: How do we want the supply chain to operate? What kind of proximity do we want to our customers? What's the engagement level we should have with the businesses and countries?

That six-month process led to basic operating principles that would guide the operation of the supply chain. Only after those principles were agreed to did they turn to the organizational chart and begin to think through how it would need to change in order for it to be aligned with the operating principles.

Examples of Design Principles of a More Global Supply Chain Organization

- Create alignment through our tailored supply chain approach to be more efficient in serving our customers.

- Refocus people on added value and simplify the country strategy through a single global supply chain point of contact at the senior vice president level

- Organize the supply chain functions and operations in order to facilitate the collaboration with businesses on the offer creation process; customer issue to prevention; sales, inventory, and operation planning; and productivity

- Present one voice to our suppliers

- Maintain a strong central function responsible for monitoring the health of the overall supply chain system

In 2013, we implemented the supply chain changes in several steps. We began by consolidating all of the supply chain functions, which were embedded in different lines of business and regions, into one global supply chain organization. The objective was for supply chain people to become "the glue" of the organization and to operate at the intersection of business strategy and country execution. Given our size and our global reach, this was a massive undertaking that involved reallocating organizational structures.

Our next step was to consolidate purchasing as a global function within the global supply chain organization, and create centers of excellence in supply chain planning, industrialization, and logistics and network design. We then integrated supply chain strategic expertise into each of the company's businesses. By doing so, we completed the transformation — leveraging scale and development of specialized competencies and identifying new leaders to oversee these competencies.

The transformation helped globalize our supply chain, which is now divided into major regions. Each region is very close to our customers, with a significant supply chain operations set-up (logistics, planning, manufacturing, and purchasing) and a consistent link to sales operations. Embedded in the businesses are our supply chain experts, bringing the business strategy to the supply chain and driving the supply chain reconfiguration to optimize scale, efficiency and customization for their customers.

A key contributor to the success of the transformation was the focus on developing talent. In 2014, we assessed more than 100 of our key supply chain leaders working in logistics, purchasing, planning, and industrialization. This exercise, which was focused on accelerating the development of our leaders, provided valuable insights on the strengths and weaknesses of each individual (and the teams they worked on) and served as a key input for the talent development roadmap.

Another key factor in the transformation effort has been the focus by supply chain leaders on promoting a learning culture across the organization. When developing the training curriculum that's offered each year, the learning and development team leveraged the data gathered during the annual talent development reviews and then confirmed this data with supply chain executives. This collaboration has played a critical role in ensuring both buy-in from the business and that the content stays relevant even amid rapid changes in the business climate.

Advantages from the transformation

The transformation has delivered a range of benefits that are beyond our expectations. In the broadest sense, it has enhanced our ability to become a trusted partner to our customers — a development that helps us create long-term relationships that drive long-term advantage. But we've also been able to measure the benefits. From 2012 through 2014, the transformed supply chain reduced customer dissatisfaction on deliveries by double digit percentages and raised the company's service level performance significantly. It also improved the amount of industrial productivity by generating cumulative savings of over €1 billion. These achievements underscore our belief that the supply chain should not be viewed as merely a cost center — it is a differentiator and a key driver of competitive advantage.

The supply chain transformation has also delivered stronger differentiation and performance in three additional areas.

First, we are now measuring our lead time exactly as customers see it. End to end, customer order to delivery. So we now move to the customer-centric measurement of success. Second, we are working on accelerating our new product introduction timelines. And third, we look for specific supply chain capability to help our smaller enterprises grow faster.

While the implementation has been a success, there were some internal challenges. Some of our leaders wanted to preserve their autonomy and were very concerned that the changes we were implementing would stifle entrepreneurial focus. While we believed that embedding supply chain strategic expertise into the businesses would translate to a single voice on supply chain issues, some in the country and different lines of businesses thought this meant relinquishing control. There were some tough conversations with those who resisted the changes, but we could always go back to the principles of what we were trying to accomplish for our customers.

Digitization of the supply chain

Starting in 2013, we began to place heightened emphasis on digitization as a way to accelerate and intensify the company's transformation. For the supply chain, this meant synchronizing suppliers' plants, distribution centers and transportation carriers, with a focus on improving service to customers. Many programs were launched in order to improve the responsiveness in relation to market demand supported by new technologies.

As part of our digital strategy, we adopted a cloud-based planning tool which is enabling the digitization of industrial demand and supply planning. The technology facilitates interaction loops between the different functions, across multiple ERPs, and improves our responsiveness to customers and suppliers and significantly reduces the value of capital engaged in inventory.

We have also digitized a large part of our relationship with our downstream customers and upstream suppliers. This creates greater transparency between stakeholders of the supply chain, including our relationships with distributors, who are also service providers.

Enabling growth for us and others

We have 45,000 suppliers and they are fundamental to our competitiveness in quality, customer service, costs, cash consumption, and our ability to innovate. They are also critical to our supply chain strategy, representing 60-70 percent of our cost of goods sold. We have engaged a digitization program with our selected suppliers to bring real-time transparency to our relationship, which helps us adapt to demand changes faster and more effectively, while reducing costs and cash consumption.

As we have grown as a company, many of our suppliers have grown alongside us and become global enterprises. Many of them have helped us navigate local rules and regulations that we need to follow as we have worked to get closer to our customers. When we encountered suppliers who were not interested in globalizing, we moved on to others, because we knew that we needed global suppliers as we transitioned from being a trans-Atlantic business to a global business.

In order to foster mutual understanding with our suppliers, we bring together several hundred top performers each year. We tell them about our company strategy and our goals. We hold workshops for example on sustainability and supply planning, and we provide training on how to leverage lean work practices to drive efficiency and quality. We also tell them about our new products and our new solutions, which we find sparks ideas from them about further innovation. This sharing of information has made us more successful in adopting innovations over the past several years.

Using big data and analytics to improve the supply chain

For the first time in the company's history, we now have comprehensive end-to-end digital information about our supply chain and how it is operating. This information is creating a huge "data lake" that is full of operating insights and opportunities, and helping us to sense, respond, and react before we see supply chain interruptions. We leveraged the data to prevent several crises with our electronic suppliers, leveraging a drastic improvement of the visibility, reliability and alignment of the forecasts of our own needs, of the suppliers' production plan, and of the intermediary inventory levels. The true heroes in supply chain prevent supply chain interruption for our customers and we are moving swiftly in that direction.

Fundamental to this progress has been strong collaboration with our critical suppliers. We are now beginning to use this tool with key customers as well, such as distributors, which represents the next step in our efforts to deepen collaboration with our external partners, downstream and upstream.

We have also developed a powerful tool that is giving us greater visibility into our global inventory. It is extracting massive amounts of data from enterprise resource planning and synthesizing this data into actionable reports, for every manufacturing and distribution location. We are able to measure the "healthy" stock (that which will be useful to meet future demand from our customers), the obsolete stock, the extra inventory, and the missing inventory we have to recover.

We are also using data in connection with the deployment of our logistics network modeling tool throughout the company. Starting with research on customer delivery needs, we simulate our network of distribution in order to propose the best combination of customer lead time offer, relevant flows, inventory locations, cost and cash. Once it is calibrated to represent the real life of our "order to deliver" flows, we can simulate the future flows and predict how our supply chain will adapt to these buying behaviors. Starting with a pilot in 2011, we redesigned our logistic network in Australia, China, Brazil, and have been progressively redesigning the worldwide network.

Our talent challenge

Attracting, developing, and retaining talent is fundamental to our supply chain strategy. We review the talent pool and the pipeline at least twice each year, and a dedicated talent management team for the global supply chain organization plans, manages, and tracks progress against the talent agenda. We maintain a Global Supply Chain Academy, which addresses competency gaps across our supply chain organization with a comprehensive and robust curriculum, while leveraging e-learning to drive global reach and scale. All of this work is carried out in close collaboration with our supply chain leaders and our human resources team.

One encouraging indicator is that our global supply chain organization is now perceived as an important stop for business leaders in career development. And for the first time in the company's history, front-office talent is asking for key roles in supply chain to broaden their experience. Key supply chain leaders are also being sought for line-of-business roles, reflecting that the global supply chain organization is now a vital pool of talent for the broader company.

Our focus on the supply chain as a source of advantage, and a tool to deepen the partnership with customers, has improved our ability to attract the best people. Supply chain professionals see us as a place where they can be in the supply chain today and run a line of business tomorrow. It's a great opportunity for them and it certainly helps us when we're recruiting them.

We are proud to have seen progressive improvement in the profile of our workforce. We have a stronger pool of diverse talent globally compared to just a few years ago, and in many countries the leadership talent is primarily local, and the company's reliance on international assignees has declined by over 30 percent.

Top three challenges

Looking ahead, we see three management challenges connected to supply chains.

First, digitization is changing the way supply chains operate as well as the competencies that are required inside the supply chain. The real winners in supply chain strategy will be those companies that can optimize the supply chain beyond their own borders — reaching into their customers and their suppliers and leveraging the end-to-end space. Companies that take these steps will be more agile than their competitors and more attractive to potential customers.

A second challenge will be the talent shortage in the supply chain space, particularly attracting diverse talent. There aren't enough students studying supply chain curriculums and the average age of supply chain professionals is rising. As more and more companies adopt supply chain as a competitive advantage the shortage of talent is growing. As a result, companies are going to need to professionalize talent, develop it and, most importantly, retain it.

The third challenge, specific to Schneider, will be developing and combining the best of breed of digital tools in all supply chain domains (Planning, Manufacturing, Logistics, Purchasing) together with the traditional ERPs. This will make it possible to obtain a superior orchestration of our supply chain, to the delight of our customers while saving costs and cash and ensuring a high level of reliability and agility.

The next 10 years

I foresee a number of changes to supply chains in the decade ahead.

For starters, they will become even more digitized. For customers, this will translate to more and more "easy to use" and intuitive functionalities. Underpinning the digital orchestration of the overall supply chain will be a sophisticated and efficient integration of best of breed IT tools, covering a vast ecosystem of functionalities and connected to multiple internal and external partners.

Next, we will also see a greater integration of the supply chain with other business functions, such as marketing. The supply chain will likely be seen as "the place," which is one of the four P's of marketing (the others being price, product, and promotion). Most industrial companies will rediscover that supply chains can be a tremendous competitive advantage in the marketplace.

Additionally, supply chains will also be more tailored to customer needs and will be a source of differentiation, helping users understand and satisfy the different customer buying behaviors.

Sustainability will also assume a more prominent place in the supply chain agenda, given the growing focus on issues such as resource scarcity and climate change. This growing commitment by companies to sustainability, and the demands it places on an enterprise's supply chain approach, will provoke new ways of doing things and help bring innovation to the surface along the supply chain. It will bring a greater need of research for efficiency, as well as systems that integrate the full equation of efficiency that is linked closely to energy utilization and process productivity.

Finally, with the growing recognition of the supply chain driving both cost and competitive advantage, expectations of what the supply chain can deliver will continue to grow.

Conclusion

One of our bedrock business principles has always been that life is short, so one must innovate. That principle guided the transformation of our supply chain — an undertaking that has helped us realize greater agility and efficiency, and most importantly, serve our customers more effectively. And we've upended the thinking about our supply chain, which far from being a cost center is helping to deliver top-line growth.

And true to the bedrock principle, as much as our supply chain has improved, we also realize that we can't stand still — the improvements and innovations must keep coming if we are going to maintain our long-term advantage and deliver differentiated value to our customers and the marketplace.

A 20-Year Arc of Rapid Change and Innovative Disruption

Jerry Yang

I have a keen appreciation for the power of disruption because I experienced it at an early age. I was born in Taiwan, but at the age of 10, I moved with my mother and my brother to northern California. I barely spoke English at the time, but that rapidly changed — as did everything else in my everyday life. About eight years later, in 1986, I was admitted to Stanford University, from which I graduated in 1990.

A few years after finishing college, while pursuing graduate work in electrical engineering at Stanford, I joined with one of my fellow students, David Filo, to create a comprehensive directory of websites. Keep in mind, we could be comprehensive because this was 1994 — very much the early days of the World Wide Web (there were fewer than 3,000 websites in existence). But that directory evolved into a company, and the next big disruption in my life was taking a leave from Stanford in 1995 to incorporate the company, which we called Yahoo!, and we celebrated its 20-year anniversary this year!

Nineteen-ninety-five was not just a big year for me. It was also the year when the Internet — the most disruptive consumer technology since the automobile — started to go mainstream. One of the seminal moments that year was the Netscape IPO on August 9. It was the first Internet-oriented company to go public, and on the first day of trading it closed with a valuation of close to $3 billion, despite having released its first web browser less than a year earlier.

That was a starting point for a remarkable pattern of innovation and disruption that followed — a 20-year arc of rapid change, with roughly five-year cycles of innovative disruptions. And the pattern has been pretty continuous ever since, drawing on the World Wide Web, social networking, and mobile computing and communications. While there have been bubbles and downturns, each cycle has sparked more innovation, and brought more pervasive change to the pace and connectedness of our daily lives. Companies like Google, which was incorporated in 1998, emerged stronger from the first downturn — in 1999-2000 — because they were able to disrupt more established players who had to retrench. Similarly, amid the steep economic and market downturn in 2008-09, a new breed of companies emerged, or were born, that disrupted existing markets — or created entirely new ones: Facebook (founded in 2004), Twitter (2006), Airbnb (2008) and Uber (2009). Nor was this cycle restricted to Silicon Valley and the United Sates. China entered the scene with companies like Tencent, Baidu, Alibaba and now, Xiaomi.

While the innovation of the last 20 years has been driven primarily by information technology in both the consumer and enterprise space, the advent of smartphones, the cloud, and other core technologies have transformed the landscape and catapulted the growth of software, as well as what is now frequently referred to as the "app economy." As a result, the PC has been replaced by the mobile device as the center of gravity for individual access to technology usage and the Internet.

In this chapter, I discuss the disruptive innovations of today and tomorrow, and touch on a number of related themes, such as managing disruptive innovation, the types of individuals who succeed at it, and threats to it. But first, I want to focus on what may be the most profound change in technology over the past ten years: China's ability to differentiate itself as a creator of innovation.

Innovation and the Internet in China

One of the most transformative developments in the global economy has been the continued rise of China. I have followed this progress with particular interest, given my Chinese background. Yahoo! started operating in China in 1999 and during one of my trips to the country two years earlier, I had the good fortune to be given a tour of the Great Wall by a very impressive former English teacher, named Jack Ma, who was just a few years older than me. He was very curious about the Internet and what its future might be. He told me he planned to start an e-commerce company to serve the Chinese market, and I was impressed with his ambition. We stayed in contact in subsequent years. We followed the company Jack founded, called Alibaba, which charted extremely impressive growth. In 2004, it had $50 million in revenue, and by the following year it had 2,400 employees. In May 2005, I traveled to China with three of my colleagues — the CEO, Terry Semel; the President, Sue Decker; and development executive Toby Coppel — and we met with the company's executives. Upon our return, we were in agreement that Yahoo! should invest in Alibaba, and this year, 2015, marks the 10-year anniversary of that investment.

A few months after the trip, in August, we announced a $1 billion investment, coupled with the $700 million in assets from Yahoo! China. The investment, which triggered some skeptical commentary from outsiders, gave Yahoo! 40 percent ownership of the company. Alibaba continued to achieve meteoric growth and in September 2014 it sold $25 billion worth of shares on the New York Stock Exchange. It was the largest initial public offering ever.

In the decade since Yahoo!'s investment, Alibaba's growth has been emblematic of the evolution of China's Internet economy. Going back to the year 2000, China was well behind the rest of the world. Less than two percent of the population had access to the Internet, connections were slow, and the government blocked select content. As more people gained access to the Internet in the years that followed, the number of Internet-oriented companies in the country grew, though they were largely "copycats" of successful companies that had been founded elsewhere. There were few "true" home-grown innovations, which did not change much until about 2010.

But in the past five years, China-based Internet companies have achieved even more remarkable differentiation and growth. The country's entrepreneurs have been creating disruptive technologies that are not just copycats. Indeed, they are often out-innovating their Western counterparts. In addition to Alibaba, there are highly successful companies like Baidu (an Internet search provider) and Tencent (an Internet communications and services portal). In terms of market cap, they rival U.S. companies like Facebook and Amazon.

One particularly innovative Chinese company is Xiaomi, which develops and distributes apps, smartphones, and other consumer electronics products. The company has leveraged its own operating system and app store, along with an integrated suite of services, to develop a loyal following. Here's how *Wired* magazine has described Xiaomi's appeal:

> Xiaomi is quickly building a connected hardware ecosystem that includes TVs, WiFi routers, and an air purifier, offering a glimpse of what the world might have looked like if Apple rather than Google had bought Nest. Anchored by its phones and MiUI, Xiaomi offers a model of an integrated system where consumers don't have to puzzle through how to connect up the various devices in their homes. Everything just connects up to the platform already at the center of their lives.[1]

By the summer of 2015, there were 40 million members of Xiaomi's user forums, and to deepen their connection with the company, they are consulted in advance of operating system updates. While only founded in 2010, Xiaomi sold more than 60 million smartphones in 2014 — more than any company in the world after Apple and Samsung.

Chinese companies like Xiaomi are clearly transitioning China from "fast follower" status to parallel development. With an estimated 650 million Chinese online (twice as many as people who live in the United States), there's high upside potential for Internet-oriented companies. The investment bank Morgan Stanley has estimated that by 2018, there will be more online transactions in China than in the rest of the world combined.[2]

But like any market, China is not without its tricky aspects. Set against the extraordinary opportunities is a discomforting reality: any Internet-oriented company — whether domestic or foreign — is at risk of having the central government block some or all of its offerings. Today, a number of sites that are popular around the world — including Twitter, Facebook, Instagram, and YouTube — are difficult to access in China. And in 2010 Google withdrew from mainland China and shifted to Hong Kong amid concerns that its search results were being censored. On the other hand, some companies have fared quite well there. China is a major market for Apple, and the CEO, Tim Cook, has said the country is on track to generate more revenue for the company than the United States.

But companies operating in China must recognize that the innovation and growth of the Chinese Internet market go hand-in-hand with understanding and dealing with very complicated government influences and regulations. The Chinese government is emblematic of what Chris Caine referred to in his chapter — it can be your biggest ally or your biggest adversary.

Today — and tomorrow
Current trends
The progress in China is one element of a larger global story that is still being written about the golden age of innovation that's underway.

In just the past three years, I've focused my efforts on to investing and helping entrepreneurs create the next high-impact, disruptive companies. What I have seen is that we are experiencing a surge of innovative disruption in four key technology sectors: cloud computing, commerce transactions, mobile, and "engagement." The way in which each of these are developing is fundamentally different relative to past breakthroughs of just 5-10 years ago.

Consider how messaging has become the new platform for engagement – at the expense of search and of email. More specifically, consumer engagement on mobile devices has surpassed engagement via the traditional devices like laptops and PCs. Engagement is an important concept for consumer Internet companies because whoever can "own" the most consumer engagement will have the best chance to bundle and sell more services to the consumer. While Internet-era engagement platforms started with AOL, followed by Yahoo!, then Google, and then Facebook, the leaders now are U.S.-based entities like WhatsApp (which had 700 million monthly active users as of January 2015) and Snapchat, as well as the China-based WeChat. The companies are taking different approaches. For example, WeChat is becoming the most pervasive messaging platform in China. In addition to a rich offering of entertainment, games, and commerce, WeChat is also in some cases replacing email in the workplace. At the other end of the spectrum, WhatsApp is a simple, no-frills app that only focuses on fast, simple messaging, primarily allowing people to send texts for free.

While engagement is an evolving space, it's clear that whoever has the most engagement has the greatest competitive advantage. The historical analogy is the television era and advertising. As Shelly Lazarus highlights in her earlier chapter, the company with the most viewers has the opportunity to provide users with more services and generate more revenue. But not all markets place the same emphasis on advertising as a financial and business model. As *The Economist* pointed out in July 2015,

> Chinese firms are inventing new business models. The West's on-line firms generate most of their revenue from advertising. But China's advertising industry is only about one-eighth the size of America's, so Chinese digital firms have had to find new ways to

monetize their users' eyeballs. Tencent generates 90% of its revenue from online games, sales of virtual items on social platforms and e-commerce. Average revenue per user in 2014 was $16, which was $6 more than Facebook. YY.com, an online-video platform, lets viewers buy electronic "roses" to shower upon video artists whose shows they enjoyed. YY says its top performers, who get a cut of the revenue, can earn more than 20,000 yuan ($3,200) a month, seven times the average factory worker's pay.[3]

Beyond engagement, the largest driver for disruption is the emergence of the big-data economy. This trend has been precipitated by technologies like cloud computing and storage taking over the enterprise ("software as a service" taking over traditionally purchased hardware and licensed and installed software), mobile technologies (being the new catalyst and platform for enabling new industries such as the sharing economy), and information technology tools that drive commercial action by instantly matching demand with supply, as opposed to just generating information (this is frequently referred to as "being Uberized").

The big-data economy takes advantage of tremendous amounts of data being generated by mobile devices, transactions, locations, and consumers' actions. The data are then aggregated (mostly in the cloud), and computation can be applied to analyze and derive insights that are useful. The more useful the insights, the better the future data that is collected. From there, companies that fully leverage big data find the virtuous cycle. Big data and analytics have begun migrating to virtually every industry and are being utilized by managers in fundamental ways to help them increase their efficiency and position themselves for a very different economic era.

The advent of new core technologies is the basis for continued growth and innovation in more conventional IT industries. However, we are witnessing a broader, more exciting trend of these technologies being merged into other industries and helping to create entirely new potential for innovation and disruption. Biologists, biochemists, and geneticists are teaming up with data scientists and computational scientists to create next-generation companies around life science. Young companies are being formed around drug discovery using big data, as well as the use of biology, combined with databases, to create proteins to replace meat and eggs.

Entrepreneurship itself also is changing rapidly. Young, enterprising entrepreneurs are fast combining deep domain expertise with other disciplines. There are many examples of this, and they underscore the explosion of applied innovation that is underway. A number of other industries that people did not associate with IT 10 years ago are also being infused with information-data characteristics and being taken in new and exciting directions: medicine and hospitals, food and agriculture, financial services, and robotics and space, just to name a few.

The cloud is also enabling faster and better products and services. Among the many efficiencies the cloud offers, it organizes businesses with far fewer interruptions in service and carries out releases at any time. Gone are the days of distributing changes in tangible packages and waiting for installation (a scenario that was commonplace in the past, with CDs containing software upgrades being mailed to customers). These changes have created accelerated flows of products and features. Hand-in-hand with this come subscription business models, rather than the license business model — a development that is fundamentally changing the enterprise software business. And perhaps the most noted examples outside of the technology sector, companies like Uber and Airbnb are disrupting the transportation and hotel industries. In the process, they're creating not only new disruptive business models but also new micro-economic models.

We are also seeing the construction of physical warehouses for last-mile distribution connected to delivering on-demand product orders. Drones are being sent on deliveries to shorten fulfillment time and capture the attention and loyalty of customers and potential customers. These developments and investments are being driven by a structurally different enterprise environment than just 10 years ago — an environment that is placing a premium on access to real-time data, speed and precision, and the ability to store and retrieve historical data for more intuitive future decision-making. Incumbent businesses, if they are going to compete, must tear down their traditional operating models and cost structures and integrate these new tools — and even more important — integrate new thinking.

Another trend that is unleashing exciting innovations is the merging of hardware and software. This breaks with the pattern of the past 30 years, which has been driven by horizontal players. Companies were either focused on building hardware, or they supplied software to run on someone else's hardware. The "Wintel" era marked by Microsoft and Intel allowed software companies to focus on software, and hardware companies to build better computers. Steve Jobs never relinquished the idea that hardware and software should be built together. He talked about it as early as 1980, and his idea was eventually embodied in the iMac and then the iPhone.

Today, the prevailing idea is that hardware and software done right together can create more value. More traditional horizontal players, like Microsoft, Oracle, and Intel are trying to catch up to this trend. In June 2015, Microsoft merged its hardware and software divisions, and labeled the new division the "Windows and Devices Group." The Internet of Things is also driving this change, with highly-talented hardware and software professionals collaborating in sectors ranging from medical devices to home automation. The near-ubiquity of Asian contract manufacturers allows great software and hardware entrepreneurs to rapidly build, innovate, and scale their designs.

Areas of future disruption

One of the staples of most conversations about technology is some discussion of "the next big thing." It is a fun topic for speculation, but as I have tried to describe with the reference to the arc of innovation, there is not necessarily a single "next big thing." However, having observed many entrepreneurs recently, there are common attributes that make possible the "next big thing." One attribute of the "next big thing" is the boldness of the idea. Whether it is curing cancer, going to Mars, or creating smart cars and robots, "big thing" ideas are *boldacious* and frequently provoke disbelief. Another attribute is the degree of disruption to the status quo. Big ideas are often executed against the tide of conventional wisdom. A third and final attribute is timing — while most big ideas are ahead of their time, they cannot be too far ahead. Often these ideas catch on, have network effects, and create their own ecosystem. In an increasingly connected world, the next "big thing" can come from anywhere. I, for one, will be observing with anticipation!

As such, we should expect continued disruptive innovation. New technology developments in computing, material science, and life sciences will continue to drive today's "golden age of innovation." 3-D printing, for example, may transform manufacturing and supply chains, since products can be manufactured on demand, virtually anywhere, and price differentials will shift from the traditional processes of production and distribution to design. Is it possible that car companies will no longer need to manufacture millions of spare parts and store them, since these parts could be manufactured locally and only when customers need them?

I also see change ahead in the area of supply chains — a theme Jean-Pascal Tricoire explores in the previous chapter. Many people view the complexity of supply chains and can only see that there are multiple points of potential failures. Through my investing, I have begun to see a new perspective emerge — one that treats supply chains as similar to other large, complex systems, with real-time information and big data enabling the identification of patterns, and the ability to predict potential disruptions. Thus a storm in one part of the world that threatens to interfere with a supply chain could trigger immediate adjustments to a company's workflow. The net effect is, as Tricoire points out, for the supply chain to evolve from a cost center to a source of competitive advantage.

I see additional positive societal benefits connected to disruptive innovation, particularly in the areas of medicine and health. Consider drug discovery. Traditionally, researchers would have to mix chemicals and agents to ensure the drug works. That would be a two-year cycle. But if you can use big data to reduce that to six months, the business model implications are huge for management and business developers. Think about the potential of delivery drones cost-effectively delivering emergency medicine to people in remote or inaccessible places. And think about the realm of personalized medicine, which is a huge societal and economic opportunity. If every iPhone can be a pretty good doctor, for diagnostics, individuals can be the first line of defense for their own health. That will change the medical system. People have not wrapped their heads around this yet, but they will soon.

There are two other areas where I see significant innovation ahead. While some technology experts are projecting an end to Moore's Law, and therefore the IT revolution that it enabled, this view overlooks a number of other ways in which IT can drive innovation, disruption, and growth. Quantum computing, for example, is not driven by the speed of semiconductors, and the difference with traditional, semiconductor-driven computing is almost literally night and day. As a writer for *Fast Company* has described it, "A quantum computer harnesses the science of the very small — the strange behavior of subatomic particles —to solve problems that are computationally infeasible for a classical computer or simply take too long."[4] In the next decade, quantum computing can potentially be commercialized and computing will be revolutionized in ways that are difficult to comprehend.

The other area ripe for innovation is artificial intelligence. Theoretical ideas that were discussed in AI classes two or three decades ago are now starting to happen in real life. It will not be long before tasks we associate with high intelligence will be performed better by machines than by humans. For instance, there is already a lot of discussion about the self-driving car. AI and deep learning techniques are increasingly pervasive in learning applications. I expect AI will fundamentally change the way we work, live, and perpetuate ourselves.

Success Factors and Captains of the Future

In our technology-obsessed world, I believe the single most important component of innovation and disruption is, and will remain, the individual. The best idea for a new business or product will not go anywhere without highly-capable people working to turn that idea into something viable.

I now spend my time identifying and supporting new entrepreneurs and ideas. When we make investments, the dominant criteria for our decision is driven by the individual or team that's been assembled to implement the idea. Talent is everything. And one of the under-appreciated qualities we look for in our entrepreneurs is an ability to pivot. Very few initial ideas for a business plan remain intact through its life.

The top companies in my portfolio are all doing something very different today than what they said they would be doing when we invested in them years ago. This is for me the most important attribute for determining a successful company in this environment of accelerating innovation. Does the group of people who have an idea and want to bring that idea to the world have the temperament and resilience to go in a different direction if and when it will be needed? If yes, they have a good chance for success. If no, the outlook is dim because the pace of change is accelerating — and will continue to do so.

There is nothing obvious about pinpointing entrepreneurs who will be successful. Indeed, it is particularly difficult because good entrepreneurs are, by definition, unorthodox. They see things differently than everyone else. Sometimes that translates to failure. Other times it means success. That said, we look for people who have a track record of entrepreneurial success or have worked at companies during high-growth phases. But the rules are hardly set in stone. The founder of Snapchat, Evan Spiegel, had no background as a disruptive entrepreneur. Nor did Facebook CEO Mark Zuckerberg.

Similarly, if you looked at Jack Ma on paper, you would not say he fits the stereotype of an entrepreneur. He is not a technologist, nor trained in product or tech. Yet he is a charismatic leader and someone who can inspire — whether one-on-one or when speaking to a full stadium of customers. He is also a visionary. He sees a future for Alibaba, and can tell the story to inspire others to join the cause. Jack's strength is in assessing and developing talent — he is relentless in his focus on developing his organization, and building strength in the ranks. He is intensely competitive and focused on where the future of his enterprises are going. It comes as no surprise that despite their background, origin, or age, entrepreneurs from around the globe share similar traits.

Management in an Era of Disruptive Innovation

A common topic of discussion in Silicon Valley and elsewhere is whether the CEOs of large technology companies must be "product-driven" to succeed. I think this debate obscures an even more important question: do the CEO and senior managers have a mindset that's focused on innovation?

In the not-so-distant past, management was largely about cost-cutting while also achieving "efficiencies" and "synergies." While those are still important, they're not sufficient. Today, CEOs need to be relentless in their pursuit of a vision for improving the customer experience through innovation. That vision needs to become embedded in the company's DNA. Relying on a siloed team of innovators to develop "the next big thing" is a risky — and probably unsustainable — strategy. Successful business leaders need to construct and nurture an innovative mindset enterprise-wide, as that's the only way a company will be able to not only respond to change, but drive it.

The Disruptions That Could Derail Disruptive Innovation

While I am very optimistic about a future "that innovation enables," I also recognize that there's no guarantee that it will be as pervasive in this century as it was in the previous one. Indeed, there are a number of factors that could disrupt repeated arcs of innovation.

One looming issue relates to data and data protection. Data is fundamental to online activity and, by extension, the ideas that underpin innovation. But a critical question has emerged in recent years: Who owns data once it's online? And who has the right to access it? There are no simple answers to these questions, as we've seen in the past few years. And there are no international standards outlining what governments can, and cannot, access. Nor is it clear whose data can be accessed.

Consider the following questions: Is a government of one country prohibited from accessing the data of a citizen of another country? What about a company headquartered in another country? For data stored in the cloud, does that data sit in any country? Here's a purely hypothetical scenario that speaks to the data regulation challenge: The Japanese subsidiary of an American company, with a CEO from Mexico, stores its data using servers that are based in the Netherlands. Would authorities representing all of these countries have jurisdiction over the stored data? If not, why not?

Cybersecurity poses a similar threat to disruptive innovation. There is an arms race underway, with massive investments being made to secure systems that are still being penetrated by hackers throughout the world — some of whom appear to have ties to governments. While there are measurable costs of security breaches, what cannot be measured are the long-term costs that stem from potential innovations being interrupted — and perhaps never pursued — because security is compromised.

While it is unlikely these issues will ever be fully resolved, the costs can be minimized through concerted and coordinated action by the public and private sectors. Absent that action, there is going to be a gradual erosion of trust in everything related to the Internet. The ripple effect from that erosion of trust would not only undermine continued innovation but also threaten future societal and economic benefits.

Conclusion

The writing of this chapter coincided with the 20th anniversary of a seminal moment at Yahoo! — the day we put advertising on the site: August 1, 1995. While that decision seems elementary today, at the time many considered it heresy. We did not know if we would alienate our most loyal users with such a move. But advertising was our lifeline — it created a revenue stream that enabled us to achieve everything that followed.

That episode is a reminder that the power of disruptive innovation comes not just from the marriage of good ideas to powerful technology — the third and fourth legs of the stool are a business model that attracts paying customers and a management model that keeps the company focused on its core idea and flexible enough to pivot when the core idea needs to change. I have seen many disruptive ideas go nowhere because the people behind them have not been able to build a market for them and manage the inevitable transitions related to them.

This is the part of innovation that does not attract as much attention. While the success stories tend to dominate the headlines, for every success there are often many companies that pursued the same idea but failed. That is a reminder of something that should be obvious but sometimes gets overlooked: innovation is not easy. Indeed, it is almost always excruciatingly difficult. The odds are always against the innovator, which is why it takes a distinctive kind of personality to succeed. As the Irish playwright (and co-founder of the London School of Economics) George Bernard Shaw once wrote, "The reasonable man adapts himself to the world; the unreasonable one persists in trying to adapt the world to himself. Therefore all progress depends upon the unreasonable man."

I am optimistic that the world will continue to see a steady stream of "unreasonable" men — and women — to ensure that the march of human progress continues. The individuals have a strong foundation from which to draw, given the proliferation of the core technologies I've described in this chapter. Other technologies — like quantum computing and artificial intelligence — are just around the corner. And it is almost certain that over the next 10-20 years, innovations will emerge throughout the world that give rise to benefits no one could imagine today. Thus the timeless truth expressed by computer scientist Alan Kay in 1971: "The best way to predict the future," he said, "is to invent it."

Forces of Change: Networks, Data, and Platforms

Peter C. Evans

C ompanies today are operating in a transformative period. New digital technologies, coupled with larger and more complex networks (both physical and digital), are revolutionizing the way companies innovate and operate. These changes have far-reaching implications. At the industry level, they are creating new business models, with companies disrupting old industries (from transportation to lodging) or creating entirely new ones (such as social media). At the enterprise level, they are changing the formula for value creation, with a greater premium attached to intangible assets. At the executive level, they are creating new levels of complexity but also new tools and capabilities that connect with a new knowledge infrastructure to help acquire and interpret critical information. These changes are noteworthy in two other ways: they are unfolding with extraordinary speed and they are doing so in countries of all income levels, throughout the world.

Forces of Change

Three primary forces are driving the changes that are sweeping the corporate landscape.

Age of networks

One of the forces fundamentally changing companies is the proliferation of networks. At their most basic level, networks are made up of patterns of interconnections between different things. Many networks are dedicated to moving physical goods, such as rail networks and roads or fuels like natural gas through extensive pipeline systems.[1] Other networks, like telecommunication systems, support the transfer of different forms of data, such as voice, video and computer files, from one point to another. There are also networks that support connections and interactivity between people (social media) or larger entities such as firms (business ecosystems). Thus, networks can be physical, digital or social.

A noteworthy feature of networks is that their value typically grows as they become larger, denser, and more complex. (In commercial networks this is reflected in an expansion of the number of buyers and sellers who are brought together to interact and exchange goods and services.). That growth contributes to lower costs and creates greater flexibility in the system, which in turn fosters even more growth. Economists refer to these positive spillovers as network effects.

We live in a period when many networks are growing at breathtaking speed. Twenty years ago, there were 35 million Internet users, and they accounted for just 0.6 percent of the world's population. Today, there are close to three billion Internet users, accounting for close to 40 percent of the world's population. The growth among mobile phone users during the same period is even more impressive, rising from 80 million to 5.2 billion.[2] Physical networks continue to expand as well, especially in emerging markets as their core transportation, energy, and healthcare infrastructure develops.

Indeed, much of the excitement and surge in investment activity around the Internet of Things is a byproduct of a growing share of people and machines being linked together, which will lead to more powerful network effects with expanded value propositions.

Age of data

A second force transforming the way companies operate and make decisions is the ability to access massive pools of data and sift through that data to gain real-time insights on themselves, their customers, and markets. As IBM's former Chairman and CEO, Sam Palmisano, has written, "Big Data and analytics are much more than a planning tool, and are not limited to back-office functions. They go straight to the core functions of a company: how products are designed and marketed, how decisions are made, and what actions are taken." The CEO of a data firm has made a similar point: "Ten years from now, when we look back at how this era of big data evolved, we will be stunned at how uninformed we used to be when we made decisions."[3]

One of the biggest sources of data has been (and will continue to be) web-connected devices that contain sensors, which generate information about how and when products are being used. It's projected that there will be more than 22 billion web-connected devices by 2020, which will generate more than 2.5 quintillion bytes of new data every day.[4]

Big data has become a catch-all term to describe a combination of software applications, hardware tools, and methods to capture, process, analyze and distribute data. The benefits commonly attributed to big data are that it:

- Drives cost savings

- Increases productivity gains

- Boosts innovation and discovery

- Yields deeper customer insights

- Improves profitability

Given these perceived benefits, it's not surprising that spending on big data has been growing rapidly. In 2014, the big data market was estimated to be nearly $28 billion — up from about $7 billion three years earlier — and it included spending on professional services, storage, networks and software ranging from apps and analytics to cloud and infrastructure software.[5] By 2017, the market is expected to grow to $50 billion. One indicator of the growth is the investment in big data startups. Between 2010 and 2014, more than 100 companies launched with "data" in their name, attracting $1.4 billion in investment.[6]

With more data, and more powerful tools to make sense of it, companies will be able to make decisions faster and with greater precision, and can improve upon traditional probabilistic approaches to product lifecycle management.[7] This will have profound consequences for how and where companies operate. But the growing volume and velocity of data also presents executives with a wide range of challenges. As Robert Rigobon (founder of the Billion Prices Project) has stated, the challenge is to convert data to information and information into actionable knowledge.[8]

Age of platforms

A third driver of enterprise change is the emergence of platform business models. Platforms shift the focus from a contained enterprise to ecosystems where value is created through facilitating exchange, and frequently opening themselves up to third parties who add value to the platform.[9]

Underlying these changes are business models that leverage platforms. One key feature of platform businesses is that they deliberately seek out network effects — recognizing that a virtuous cycle can be created, catapulting them to very rapid growth, once the initial chicken-and-egg problem is resolved. Jeff Bezos, the founder and CEO of Amazon, refers to this as the "Amazon flywheel."[10]

Another feature of platforms is the ability to efficiently match buyers and sellers in the market. While there is always friction associated with transactions between buyers and sellers, by building new software and harnessing the speed and scale of the Internet, platforms help reduce that friction. Innovative platform entrepreneurs have discovered that there are ways to get the flywheel going faster if one side of the market is enticed. It is not uncommon to see platforms offering deep discounts to one side of a market or even provide "freemium" goods or services to third parties to induce them to contribute and innovate on the platform.

Platforms also present very different strategic objectives than traditional frameworks for corporate strategy, which will often emphasize concepts like "lean" and "just-in-time" supply chain delivery. Platforms change what it means to lead organizations, forcing them to re-think their strategies, business models, leadership, organizational structures, and approaches to value creation and capture systems.

Platform companies can be separated into three types:

Transaction-based platforms

Transaction-based platforms are what they sound like — vehicles for commerce. An example of such a platform is eBay which provides the digital infrastructure — and the customer base — for millions of individual merchants to sell their products. While eBay is one of the oldest transaction-based platforms, there are many others, throughout the world: Baidu and JD.Com in China, Rakuten in Japan, Flipkart in India, and Zillow in the United States.

A key management issue for transaction-based platforms is how to foster efficient and smart matching and more valuable interaction between buyers and sellers on the platform. One significant innovation in this area is managing recommendations and reputations.

Platform Type:
Transactional, Integrated, Innovation

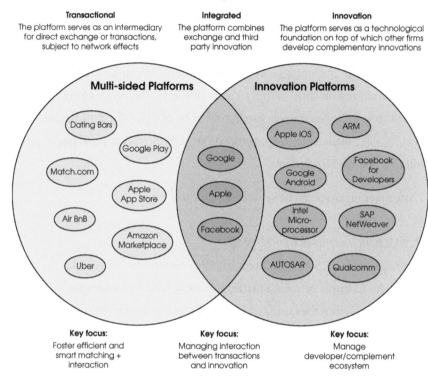

Transactional	Integrated	Innovation
The platform serves as an intermediary for direct exchange or transactions, subject to network effects	The platform combines exchange and third party innovation	The platform serves as a technological foundation on top of which other firms develop complementary innovations

Key focus:	Key focus:	Key focus:
Foster efficient and smart matching + interaction	Managing interaction between transactions and innovation	Manage developer/complement ecosystem

Source: A. Gawer and P. Evans, Platform Strategy Research Symposium, July 2015

Innovation platforms

Innovation platforms manage large ecosystems of third-party developers. Some of the bigger players in this space include Microsoft, SAP, Intel, and Salesforce.com. App stores provide one example of the value and power of open ecosystems where third parties are invited to contribute or complement the platform.

There are a number of key management questions for innovation platforms. How can they incentivize third parties to innovate on their platforms while ensuring these third parties do not infringe on their business? How can they keep their ecosystem vibrant? And what is the most effective approach to establishing and managing standards for participation on the platform?

Integrated platforms

A number of companies have succeeded in integrating both the ability to facilitate large-scale transactions as well as support large innovation ecosystems. The integration of transactions on one hand with innovation on the other create a powerful mix for growth. Companies that have brought these platform business models together include Apple, Google, Amazon, Facebook, and Alibaba. These companies not only have excelled among platforms but have, in few short years, reached ranks of the world's largest companies by market capitalization.

Platform valuations

Over the past decade, the size and reach of these three platform types has grown dramatically. As of July 2015, the world's top 50 publicly-traded platform companies had a market capitalization of about $3 trillion. They also directly employed nearly one million people, though that figure does not include Uber drivers, Airbnb hosts, or third-party developers building applications for companies like SAP, Apple, or Salesforce.com.

Publicly-Traded Platforms

Platform Type	Market Cap US $billions	Number of Employees
Integrated	1.786	347.186
Innovation	647	325.251
Transaction	593	319.724
Grand Total	3.026	992.161

Source: Global Platform Database: Center for Global Enterprise, 2015

In addition to the publicly-traded platforms, dozens of platform companies are launched each year. The startup platforms that have attracted the most attention are those that have commanded valuations of $1 billion or more — earning them the designation "unicorns." By July 2015, Uber and Airbnb had valuations of $50 billion and $25 billion, respectively. But there are many other platform-based unicorn companies. Indeed, 70 percent of unicorn companies are platforms.

In the past, it was highly unusual for any startup to have such a high valuation before going public. The success of the unicorn companies is a tribute, in part, to the power of network effects and efficient transactions. These features appeal to venture capital firms willing to place large bets on firms that can garner rapid scale, which is easier to achieve through a platform than the sale of a product. The success of some platform-based companies has also helped spur the recognition that traditional valuation models can underestimate the speed of market expansion due to network effects.

Changes over the past 10 years

There have been dramatic changes since 2005 in the three forces of change I discussed earlier (networks, data, and platforms). Much of this change has been driven by the Internet's rising speed, and expanded bandwidth, coupled with its deeper penetration into emerging markets. One emblem of the change is YouTube (now owned by Google). It was only launched in May 2005, but its expansion has been enabled by a more robust infrastructure that supports quickly uploading videos and watching them on demand. Consider that 300 hours of video are uploaded to YouTube *every minute* and half of all the views come from mobile devices.[11] Ten years ago, mobile devices were only beginning to show video and the quality was often poor.

YouTube is also an emblem of the growth of big data — a term that was coined ten years ago. In 2005, the size of the digital universe was estimated by research firm IDC to be 130 exabytes.[12] In 2014, the digital universe had grown to 4,400 exabytes.[13]

And platforms themselves have changed. While there were transaction and innovation platforms a decade ago, they've become more widespread and more comprehensive. Integrated platforms didn't exist a decade ago, but today they are a major presence. Consider Apple's App Store, it was launched in 2008, and in 2014 it generated more than $10 billion in revenue for developers, with users in 155 countries.[14]

Industry Level: Platform Disruption

The combination of deeper and more extensive networks, a greater abundance of data, and the growth of platform business models has set the stage for industry-level disruption. Publishing and music are two industries that have already felt the impact of platform companies. These mediums were particularly susceptible to digitization and instantaneous delivery over the Internet. Platforms have made inroads into new sectors, such as finance and transportation and we are seeing platform business models entering into highly-regulated industries, such as health care, finance, education, and the trading of natural resources.

The modest infrastructure needed by platform companies has enabled them to achieve global scale at extremely rapid pace. For example, Uber, founded in 2009, has a relatively small staff but operations in 58 countries and hundreds of cities. Airbnb, founded in 2008, also with few direct staff, offers listings in 180 countries and 34,000 cities. And LinkedIn, now a publicly-traded company with only 7,600 employees, has 364 million users spread across more than 200 countries and territories.

Platforms go global

The emergence of platform companies has forced a change in the traditional view of what constitutes a multinational enterprise. In the past, "multinational" typically described such globe-spanning operations as 1) natural resources extraction, which required companies to establish operations in remote locations; 2) manufacturing companies that were looking to reduce cost or move production closer to consumers; or 3) companies building large economies of scale and global brands.

An important attribute of platform companies is the ability to achieve in a fraction of time the size, scale, and global reach of traditional multinationals. The geographic scale that these digital companies have achieved is remarkable. Spotify, Uber, and Netflix now span as many countries as global giants Exxon and Rio Tinto. Airbnb helps match travelers and hosts in more places than

General Electric operates. LinkedIn and Fiverr do business in as many countries as Coca-Cola and Nestle sell their products.

And while the United States is home to a disproportionate share of highly-successful platform companies, the growth of platform companies is also being experienced in a number of other regions and countries throughout the world.

China and India

China and India are home to a growing number of platform companies. China has its own indigenous versions of all the major U.S. platform companies, and Alibaba is now one of the world's most highly-valued companies — having staged the largest IPO in history in September 2014.

China's Leading Platform Companies

China platform	US counterpart	Industry	Valuation ($B US)
Alibaba	eBay	eCommerce	192.0
Tencent	N/A	Social / Gaming	175.0
Baidu	Google	Search	64.6
JD	Amazon	eCommerce	41.0
VIP.com	Zulily, Gilt	Flash sale	19.0
Qunar	Priceline	Travel	4.7
Youku	Youtube	Video	3.6
YY Voice	N/A	Social	3.3
Weibo	Twitter	Social media	2.7
Momo	Tinder, Tingle, Blendr	Social	2.6
Renren	Facebook	Social	1.1
Tuniu	Expedia + Agoda	Travel	1.0
Zhaopin	Monster	Recruitment	0.7
Jiayuan	Match, eHarmony	Social / Matching	0.2
			511.5

Source: Weiru Chen, 2015

India is experiencing its own platform growth, which builds on the surge in mobile technology usage. One of the country's most successful platform companies, Flipkart, has announced plans to go purely mobile. And India is taking on greater significance for many leading U.S. platform firms.[15] For example, it is Facebook's second-largest market with 112 million users, WeChat's largest market with 70 million users, and LinkedIn's largest non-U.S. market with 24 million users. Other companies, such as Amazon, are quickly working to build their presence in India. In July 2014, the company announced a $2 billion investment in the country.

Additionally, both China and India have an active pipeline of platform start-ups, with a growing number having reached "unicorn" status. Together, the two countries now have 20 platform unicorns, with a combined valuation of over $72 billion and they populate a growing number of sectors — e-commerce, finance, real estate, social media, and transportation.

Africa

Platform companies have also emerged in Sub-Saharan Africa,[17] supported by an emerging middle class and strong economic growth. Once severely handicapped by the digital divide, the liberalization of the telecommunications industry and exponential growth and adoption of mobile telephony may greatly expand access to platforms. The most active sectors include e-commerce platforms, payments, and workplace. Nigeria, Kenya and Ghana have witnessed the most active platform creation and market penetration.

The two largest regional players to launch platforms are One Africa Media Group and Naspers Group. One Africa Media (OAM) operates a large portfolio of online vertical marketplaces focused on jobs, cars, property, and travel. In all, OAM serves over 400 million Africans in 11 countries, connecting buyers, sellers, employers and jobseekers. The Naspers Group is a global platform operator with interests in e-commerce, classifieds, payment, and media, and it has platform operations in all four markets. The company amassed significant amounts of capital through early and highly successful investments in Chinese Internet companies, and has expanded its operations to South America, the Middle East, Southeast Asia, Eastern Europe, and Russia.

In contrast to many regions around the world, the most active foreign platform investor in Sub-Saharan Africa is European rather than American. By far the largest and most active is Rocket Internet, a German Internet incubator. Through its regional investment arm, Africa Internet Group, Rocket Internet holds diverse consolidated interests in holding companies across the globe. Rocket's investments in Africa span e-commerce (Jumia), fashion (Zando), real estate (Lamudi), hotel bookings (Javago); jobs market (everjobs) and ride-sourcing (Easy Taxi). The majority of platforms operate within national borders and therefore have limited scale, but take full advantage of platform network effects.

Europe

The climate and outlook for platform companies in Europe is decidedly mixed. On the plus side, the region has a number of successful platform companies, such as SAP, which has a large ecosystem of third-party developers and is the world leader in enterprise applications focused on software and software-related service revenue. Other successful platform companies in Europe include Zalando, a multinational e-commerce company based in Germany that sells fashion and lifestyle products online, and Rightmove, which has become UK's largest property portal. Some other publicly-traded platform companies based in Europe include Yandex, King Digital, Markit Group, Just Eat, Criteo, Optimal Payment, Qiwi, and Zoopla.

But even on their home turf, European companies lag U.S. companies in meeting demand for platform services. Google has 90 percent market share in search in Europe; Amazon is the largest digital retailer in Europe; and the two largest mobile app stores in Europe are Google Play and Apple's App Store.

Europe also dramatically lags the U.S. as the birthplace of unicorn startups, despite a GDP that roughly equals that found in the United States and a large and active platform user base. In July 2015, there were 13 unicorn platform companies, with a valuation of $28.6 billion. The comparable figures in the United States were 42 and $191 billion. This variation in performance is one reason Europe is exhibiting signs of "platform anxiety," as evidenced by recent EU antitrust efforts directed against U.S. platform companies.[17]

Yet the EU has also launched efforts to remove barriers to platform creation and create more favorable conditions for home-grown platform development. In May

2015, the European Commission announced a "Digital Single Market" initiative,[18] which seeks to reform everything from parcel delivery to telecoms to online retailing. The initiative would also end "geoblocking," which stops consumers from buying goods or watching films from a website in another country. This effort, coupled with the proposed regulatory crackdown, reflects tension within the European Commission between officials who want to adopt a progressive model of regulation aimed at benefiting all digital companies and other officials who seek to use regulation to raise barriers against U.S. technology companies.

Can incumbents pivot?

Jerry Yang's chapter referred to the importance for managers to have resilience and the ability to change directions when needed. The rapid growth and disruptive potential of platform companies begs the question of how quickly and successfully existing enterprises can respond to platform challengers. A clue comes from the transportation sector, which until 2008 was effectively immune to platform competition. The only company to receive any venture capital investment of note from 2000 to 2008 was Zipcar, a car sharing service. But between 2008 and 2014, ride-sourcing startup companies attracted more than $4 billion in venture funding.

Investment in Ride-Sourcing Platforms, 2000 – Present

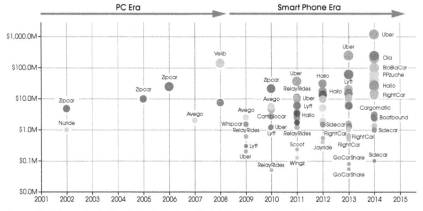

Source: Peter Evans Center for Global Enterprise, with data from CrunchBase, 2015

While considerable attention has been given to the impact of Uber on existing taxi services, established car manufacturers have also been impacted. There is a fear that an increase in ride sourcing activities could reduce the number of vehicles required in urban areas.[19] That has prompted many of the traditional automobile companies to announce ride-sourcing services of their own. One of the first was Daimler. The company's CEO, Dieter Zetsche, declared that, "We regard ourselves not only as a vehicle manufacturer but also as a provider of mobility solutions."[20]

In July 2012, the company established Moovel, an app that "shows its users the best possible way to get from A to B."[21] And in September 2014, Daimler acquired Mytaxi, a ride-sourcing platform with operations in 40 German cities as well as Washington DC, Madrid, Barcelona, Warsaw, Vienna, Graz, Salzburg and Zurich. The popularity and rapid global growth of ride-sourcing platforms have generated entirely new strategic questions. For example, should incumbents try to build platforms organically or through M&A? Similarly, should incumbents attempt to build platforms that are inclusive of other modes of transportation such as trains or even bicycles?

Enterprise Level Intangibles and Organizational Capital

The confluence of networks, data and platforms is also having important implications at the enterprise level. Some of these effects are difficult to see and measure but nevertheless are real. A striking example is the rising importance of organizational capital in how enterprises create value. Physical assets are still important, of course, but they are declining in relative importance in the overall valuation of firms.

Firms are much more than the financial capital they've earned or the physical capital they've acquired. Most important of all is often something else: their organizational capital. Resources such as equipment, labor, patents, etc., are inert by themselves.[22]

Figure 1.

Intangibles Are Growing in Value of the Enterprise

Composition of Market Value of Assets: All Public Companies

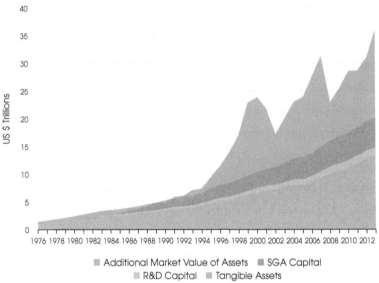

■ Additional Market Value of Assets ■ SGA Capital
■ R&D Capital ■ Tangible Assets

Organizational capital enables tangible and intangible resources, such as machines, patents, brands, and human capital to be productive. In common parlance, organizational capital is the business processes and practices that result from the following elements that drive all businesses: human capital (knowledge embodied in employees), values and norms (rules that enable the use of physical resources more efficiently), and tacit knowledge (unique business processes and practices).

Some examples of business practices that enable firms to excel are well known while others are buried deep within the enterprise. Examples include IBM's extensive system of selling or licensing knowhow; Zara's process of transmitting real time customers' choices to its suppliers worldwide; Amazon's customer recommendation system that customizes the experience for each customer; Netflix's algorithms that help customers choose their movies and TV shows; and Macy's algorithmic technology that combines online and in-store data.

Investments in intangible assets — largely organizational capital — have become significantly more important in the global and dynamic business landscape over the years. Analysis of publicly-listed companies in the U.S., for example, indicates that intangible investments have become 70 percent of the market value of U.S. corporate assets. Figure 1 decomposes the stock market value of assets, computed as the market value of equity plus the book value of debt, for all Standard and Poor's (S&P) 500 companies. The blue shaded area represents the value of assets that is not captured or adequately explained by the traditional investments in both tangible and intangible assets — much of it representing organizational capital. This unexplained portion of total value was roughly 20 percent, 35 percent, and 40 percent, respectively, until the mid-1980s and increased to 55 percent, 65 percent and 70 percent, respectively, up to 2013.

While most economists and management theorists agree that organizational capital is a key resource, frequently the agreement ends there. There are multiple approaches to the definition of organizational capital, to claims of where it resides (in employees, values and norms, enterprise knowledge, process and structure, etc.), and to the quantification (measurement) of organizational capital (input, output, survey).

Organizational capital, like other intangibles, is not captured in traditional accounting metrics. There are few guidelines for managers to measure how exactly organizational capital is created, preserved, and used to enhance the enterprise profitability, growth, and achievement of sustained competitive advantage. The organizational capital literature is in a stage akin to telling managers that R&D is important, but stopping short of how to conduct successful R&D. Accounting textbooks and discussions by accounting policymakers are seemingly blind to the existence of organizational capital.

As a consequence, CEOs are often in a quandary about what aspects of organizational capital are important, how much to invest in the various elements that make-up organizational capital, and how to communicate initiatives aimed at strengthening organizational capital to internal and external stakeholders.

Inadequate attention to measuring and managing organizational capital can have serious ramifications in the evolving business landscape of platform companies.

Executives, board members, and managers need to assess their firm's organizational capital with the impact of new disruptive technologies in mind. For example, given the ubiquitous nature of information technology, and the ways in which the "connected society" has disrupted traditional business models, managers should be asking themselves: "Do we have a good grasp on what our organizational capital is? How does our company's organizational capital help protect our existing business from disruptive technologies or new business models?"

The significance of organizational capital is even more pronounced in the case of platform companies. Companies like Uber and Airbnb create value by scaling global digital platforms that connect and match demand with supply but own few if any of these assets directly. Uber does not own the cars or employ drivers directly. Likewise, Airbnb does not own accommodations or employ hosts directly. Both companies generate value by facilitating matching and payments. As such, these companies are almost entirely based on organizational capital.

Consequently, measuring organizational capital is important to CEOs for a wide range of strategic decisions relating to internal operations, investor engagement, M&A, and alliances. Managers should:

- Track the size and growth of organizational capital and benchmark it against the past, and against rivals.

- Monitor organizational capital to avoid pitfalls such as inadequate attention to safety (BP), financial misstatements (Enron, WorldCom), and lax compliance.

- Value organizational capital, which will make it possible to assess the return on investments in creating and enhancing this resource, such as information technology (IT) and brand enhancement.

- Focus on the value of organizational capital in merger and acquisition cases, since such capital is difficult to transfer across firms, and hence should be of major concern to acquiring firms.

Example of Dell

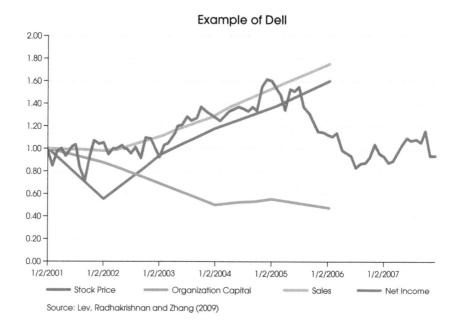

Source: Lev, Radhakrishnan and Zhang (2009)

An example may prove helpful. Dell illustrates the value of examining organizational capital. The figure above presents the sales, net income, organizational capital, and stock price data for Dell from 2001 to 2007. Sales, net income and stock price exhibit similar increasing trends from 2002 to 2005. Starting in 2005, the stock price starts to decline precipitously until the beginning of 2006, due to concerns over lack of innovation, governance practices, and accounting irregularities. The organizational capital measure shows a different trend. Starting from 2001, Dell's organizational capital measure drops off until 2004 and flattens out for 2005. This is starkly different from the backward-looking sales and net income measures, which exhibit an increasing trend during the same period. Thus the organizational capital measure provided an advance warning of Dell's operational difficulties.

The takeaway for corporate managers is simple: In a digital networked age, organizational capital is of growing importance. Companies that proactively analyze and track their organizational capital can enhance their productivity and long-term competitive advantage, as well as avoid pitfalls, such as serious safety violations or compliance shortcomings. A comprehensive measure of organizational capital also will enable companies to show investors and outside stakeholders significant value-drivers of the enterprise.

Executive Level: Data Mining, Automation, and Visual Analytics

The confluence of networks, data, and platforms is also having important implications at the executive level. The need for good information to make decisions has always been a major concern for managers. Today, the challenge is growing, as executives not only need to know what is happing within their organization but keep track of shifting conditions in the external business landscape.[23] And while executives face new levels of complexity in assessing the business and economic climate, as Michael Spence and Kevin Warsh insightfully address in the next chapter, new sets of tools and capabilities enable the development of information systems that can advance strategic decision-making.

Data search, mining, and analytics

The expanding pools of official and unofficial news provide new inputs for corporate strategy. While traditional media sources are increasingly available in digital form for direct search and analysis, new sources are continually emerging. Social media platforms like Facebook, Twitter, Google+, and blogs serve as real-time conveyers of industry news and consumer sentiment. These outlets have greatly expanded the volume of searchable information that companies need to scan and interpret. Consider that approximately four million news articles are published every day, while there are even more social media posts from millions of editorially-vetted sources across more than 100 countries, 75 languages, and 800 searchable industry topics.

The volume and variety, as well as the cost, complicates the task of integrating the information into an accessible summary. One priority has been to help companies eliminate the inefficiencies and expense of managing disparate media services, as well as simplify the way in which information is gathered, analyzed, and distributed. For example, Shell has consolidated all media and blogging into one interface intranet redesign. This automated system was embedded within Shell's intranet systems, providing Shell's employees with access to real-time news and blogs. The result is lower cost, greater productivity, and strategic business insight.[24]

As the World Wide Web has grown as a repository of news, there are limits to what can be achieved through existing approaches to news aggregation and search.[25] First, only a small portion of the total number of websites offer insights useful for market intelligence and business strategy. Second, there is a low signal-to-noise ratio. Web search results produce enormous lists of documents but they are often disconnected. There are few big data (or "big content") tools for analyzing web content for the purposes of market intelligence. Traditional search tools leave it to the user to sort through the list, which often means only a few websites get reviewed.

The next generation of tools combine media management, data mining, and analytics to improve discovery. Developed by domain experts (e.g., market intelligence professionals in the relevant industry), these tools deliver automatic relationship identification, trend analysis, and analytics that support interactive insight discovery, not batch process studies run by data scientists.

It's likely that there will be growing demand to integrate, automate, and analyze media and other sources of information critical to the enterprise. In fact, we are beginning to see rising investment in new capabilities by existing players as well as a growing number of startups with innovative ideas about how to produce the new round of innovations, such as advanced search and data automation. Companies like Quid, Northern Light, DataFox, Recorded Future, and Owlin are building such new capabilities. Companies will be able to draw on their technology to extract actionable insights from the growing volume and variation of information that is being created and distributed every day.

Visual analytics

Another valuable tool, which is only growing in importance, is visual analytics.

For years, charts, graphs and dashboards have been a standard way to synthesize and present data to managers and executives. Throughout history, there are powerful examples of graphics being used to advance business decision-making, some vivid examples of which have been captured and recorded in classic works like Edward Tufte's *The Visual Display of Quantitative Information.*[26] (Many of these were a labor of love and painstakingly drawn by hand.[27]) In the 1970s and 1980s, hand renderings gave way to computer representations. A variety of stock graphics were introduced into spreadsheet programs. PowerPoint decks with a parade of graphics from bar charts to exploding pie charts became a ubiquitous feature of business meetings. While these software programs provided basic charts reasonably well, they had a variety of limitations — such as the inability to perform more advanced visualization and the limited amount of data the programs could manage.

In the past decade, there have been significant advances in developing more sophisticated visualization tools. This has partly been driven by need, as the flood of big data has overwhelmed traditional tools. It has also been driven by a focus on connecting a growing array of database architectures and handling more complex business problems. For example, there were more than 2.6 million patents filed in 2013 and over 8.7 million were in force worldwide, with a growing number coming from new geographies such as China.[28]

Visual analytics provide a way to explore, discover, and understand not only the volume of patents but the growing complexity that arises from lawsuits, and counter-suits, claiming infringement of intellectual property, which David Kappos refers to in his chapter. This is particularly true in rapidly changing areas such as smartphones.[29] There is also demand arising from the growing complexity of other important business domain areas, such as supply chains, alliance patterns, and business ecosystems.[30] Finally, senior management has been an important driver. Executives are requesting that their strategy teams provide more sophisticated visualization to support strategic planning.[31]

Growth in advanced visual analytics has also been driven by rapidly improving capability. Innovations in computer graphics make it possible to visualize complex dynamics of firms — enhancing the ability to map out firms' relationships with each other and drive strategy. Visualization techniques also enable management and analysts to explore, discover, and understand inter-firm networks for an enterprise, specific market segments or countries, and the entire business ecosystem.

In the past, these visualization techniques were only available as custom applications developed by skilled computer scientists. More recently, there have been a growing number of standardized commercial applications that are available to enterprises. These techniques have been used to differentiate the contexts and intents of the data to be visualized. New techniques and tools are also emerging that utilize exciting new visualization and animations to visually depict a story about data that far exceeds the standard charts, graphs, and dashboards.[32] In the process, visual analytics can take data to the next step to support more sophisticated hypothesis generation, sense making, and discovery.

There has also been significant advancement in interactive visualization techniques. Instead of being limited to static graphics, interactive capabilities have introduced sophisticated ways for managers to navigate and analyze data. These navigational capabilities support a broader and more detailed view of the information. As a result, even users with little knowledge of a subject can quickly explore vast amounts of data from a wide range of perspectives. Users can also interact with interfaces or visualizations to perform a wide range of actions, including overviews, zoom, filter, search, compare, cluster, extract, order and reorder.

Dramatic advances in computing power have significantly increased the speed at which complex visualizations can be processed.[33] Interactive visualizations have even greater advantages when they connect to data that is continuously re-freshed. Visualization techniques can also build confidence in areas such as ma-chine learning (advanced pattern recognition and prediction) by demonstrating how it works through interactive visualizations of the decision trees in action.[34]

Visualizing corporate venturing

As an example, visualization can provide insight into the corporate venture activity of a company. Let's take Google. With its investment activities having expanded dramatically, a number of questions arise: Where have these invest-ments been made? What is the trend rate? Does investment flow to early or later rounds? What sectors are preferred? Where are these companies located? Visual analytics can provide a blend of rapid and comprehensive insights into these questions.

Google's investment activities have ramped up significantly as the platform has grown. In the early 2000s, the company acquired four to five companies a year on average. Between 2005 and 2009, there were more than eight acquisi-tions per year, and between 2010 and 2014 the annual average was 22.

Google's investments have covered a wide range of sectors — from payment systems, advertising and security to automation, artificial intelligence, and dig-ital platforms. The graphic below shows these sector clusters for 250 companies. There have been investments in software companies such as SurveyMonkey, Xunlei, and DeepMind (an artificial intelligence company that Google subse-quently acquired). There have also been a significant number of investments in various mobile companies, such as Apportable, which permits iOS applications (Apple) to run on Android (Google) devices automatically, without the need for changes to the underlying code. Google has also been a major investor in Uber.

While the graphic below is static, the interactive version of the data permits extensive exploration not only of macro trends but also microscopic perspec-tive, with rapid drill-downs into the details of individual companies that have received funding. Through advanced visualization, it is possible to gain insights that would be extremely time consuming, or even impossible, if using traditional approaches.

Google's Venture Funding by Company Clusters

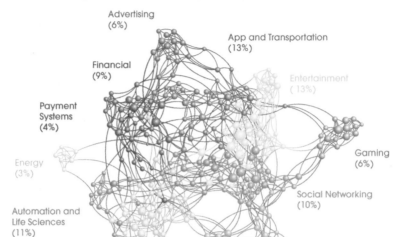

Source: P. Evans, Center for Global Enterprise, 2015

Organizational considerations

While visual analytics, data mining, and automation can deliver a number of benefits, a key management challenge is how best to align the enterprise to take full advantage of them. One approach is simply to let these capabilities evolve organically. Some companies have had enterprising analysts discover advanced visual analytic tools and drive their adoption throughout the organization. However, many companies have been less fortunate and have struggled with fully leveraging the advantages of the type of advanced analytic tools that are now available.

There are a number of ways that analytics can be brought into the enterprise. One approach is to establish a center of excellence. This consists of establishing an individual or small group that can serve as a resource to the entire organization, which helps to drive consistency and build shared knowledge across the organization. Visual analytics can also be set up as a consulting group that contracts with functions and product lines for visualization services. Another option is to decentralize visual analytics, so that functions and product lines integrate visual analytic capabilities within their units. Under this approach, the capabilities are housed directly where they will be used and therefore offer a more direct alignment between costs and benefits. The risk, of course, is that implementation may be uneven.

Just as there are no perfect visualization tools for specific projects, organizational design is likely to vary. Management teams need to consider organizational fit with existing big data and analytic initiatives, culture, and the distribution of talent. A smart approach can yield substantial rewards.

Conclusion: The Decade Ahead

Networks, data, and platforms are only going to further intensify and converge in powerful ways. Networks will continue to expand, big data is only going to get bigger, and platforms will shift from toeholds to major disrupters of a growing number of industries. Together, they will interact to shape the future business in ways that will create significant opportunities as well as risks. Various macro assessments of the Internet of Things and/or industrial Internet indicate significant opportunities. The technology and service revenue opportunity range from \$2 - \$7 trillion by 2025.[35] However, the action is going to happen at the firm level across a range of different industries.

In the coming years, value will continue to be discovered in new and unsuspected places. But it will involve being able to move upstream to where valuable data can be collected and where networks can be leveraged to establish platform leadership. The enterprises and management teams that sort this out first will be at a competitive advantage.

Another critical issue is how competition will be waged over the next decade. Recognizing that scale is important, we are seeing consortiums being formed to counteract the rising influence of the established platform companies. For example, Nokia's mapping technology was purchased by three of Germany's top carmakers — Audi, Daimler and BMW — who joined together to make the bid.[37] In South Korea, the country's three largest mobile carriers — SK Telecom, KT, and LG Uplus — announced plans to jointly establish a single app store called One Store. Their goal is to avoid fragmentation and improve their position relative to the app marketplaces of Google and Apple.[38] Meanwhile, four leading international news publishers have announced the formation of the Pangaea Alliance. The goal of this group is to consolidate online advertising inventory to better compete with global digital platforms like Google and Facebook. The alliance, made up of The Guardian, CNN International, the Financial Times and Thomson Reuters, offer advertisers the ability to access inventory (or amount of ad space a publisher has available to sell to an advertiser) across the group of top publishers through a single technology platform.[38] As value increasingly shifts towards data and platforms, we are likely to see more consortiums formed around the world in an effort to build scale and compete more effectively.

On the heels of this private-sector activity there is likely to be more attention given to platforms by governments throughout the world. Part of the effort may be aimed at removing barriers to growing platforms, as the European Commission is doing with its Digital Single Market initiative. We are also likely to see governments seek to shape the regulatory landscape in ways that could put foreign platforms at a disadvantage. There is already a trend toward governments establishing privacy and data residency rules that tilt the playing field toward local platform providers. As the value of platforms continue to grow and the stakes grow in parallel, it is likely that moves to restrict and control platforms will also grow.

In short, the forces of change that have been gathering over the past decade are likely to intensify in the decade ahead. The combination of more extensive networks, greater volumes of data, and the rise of highly successful platform business models is fundamentally altering the key success factors for leading organizations. Management teams are going to need to rethink their traditional approaches and practices, including their strategies, business models, leadership, core capabilities, value creation and capture systems, as well as organizational structures, if they are going to achieve long-term competitiveness.

Where Did the Growth Go?

Michael Spence and
Kevin M. Warsh

The global economy is struggling to grow again. In the language of most commentators, the economy has been handicapped by the financial crisis that began in 2008. We offer a somewhat different judgment. The crisis itself surely affected global growth, at least for a time. But the weakness of global economic growth during the last several years is at least as much about the post-crisis policy response as the proverbial hangover from the crisis itself.

Both developed and developing economies are expanding at slower rates than they did in the pre-crisis era. And at much slower rates than economists, central banks, and multilateral economic institutions forecasted in recent years. After years of overestimating global growth, the International Monetary Fund (IMF) threw in the towel in April 2015. It projected that growth rates for the next six years will be significantly lower than they were during the last six.

The United States and China — the two largest economies in the world — are emblematic of the global economic malaise. Growth in the U.S. averaged a meager 2.1% in the 23 quarters following the recession's trough in June 2009. And China's official growth rate in 2014 was its lowest in any year since 1990. Its actual growth rate appears to be decelerating this year.

There are varied reasons for the sluggish growth in both countries. Most frequently, we are told about the shortfall in aggregate demand. In this chapter, we focus on other factors to account for such modest performance. In the U.S., we highlight the decline in capital investment and deficiencies in public sector investment trends. In China, we discuss the country's low consumption rates and the inevitable challenges it confronts in its transition to middle-income status.

In both countries, policymakers should resist the post-crisis temptation to manage short-term fluctuation in the real economy and financial markets. They should adopt a medium-term perspective, and establish substantive policies to accomplish their growth objectives.

Time will tell whether policymakers in the United States, China, and other countries can instill a climate that is more conducive to higher economic growth over the medium-term, but globally integrated enterprises (GIEs) do not have the luxury of waiting. Business leaders must operate in the world that is, not the world in which they wish it would be. Now more than ever, they must develop a comprehensive understanding of economic trends – local, national, regional, and global – and they should engage with policymakers to press for much-needed reforms as a catalyst for higher growth.

The investment shift from real assets to financial assets

Real assets and financial assets have traditionally tracked each other reasonably well.[1] Sometimes, improving financial asset prices (in the S&P 500, for example) portend better real economic conditions to come. Other times, improvements in the real economy — better data on consumption, investment, trade, for example — augur higher financial asset prices.

Since the depths of the financial crisis, however, the performance of financial assets and real assets diverged. U.S. corporate profits and operating cash flow strengthened during the current recovery, at least until very recently. High levels of profits and cash flow were aided by improved growth, lower interest rates, cost savings, and productivity improvements.

This explains, in part, the significant share price appreciation from 2009 through the end of 2014. Extremely accommodative monetary policy, including quantitative easing (QE), meaningfully supported this rise in the value of risk-assets.

If history were a guide, that should have translated to significant investment in real assets. High share prices tend to be highly correlated with increased business confidence and higher capital expenditures. But when comparing business investment patterns during this cycle to history, the results are highly anomalous. Broad measures of fixed investment, as a share of GDP, have retreated since the financial crisis. Private investment (net of depreciation) was $524 billion in 2013 — but it was $860 billion in 2006. And while U.S. GDP rose 8.7% from late 2007 through 2014, gross private investment was just 4.3% higher. The growth in non-residential fixed investment remains substantially lower than the last six post-recession recoveries.

The trend is not encouraging. In the second quarter of 2015, non-residential fixed investment declined 0.6%. During the final quarter of 2014, and the first two quarters of 2015, non-residential investment only grew 0.6% at an annual rate. That is barely enough to cover depreciation. Investment in structures declined 1.6%. Investment in equipment declined at an annual rate of 2.2%. Only a 6.5% increase in software kept overall investment positive.

So, where is the money?

Russell 1000 companies (outside of financials) devoted more than 70% of free cash flow to buybacks in 2014, up from just 45% in 2010.[2] In fact, 2014 was the first year since 2007 that companies spent more money on buybacks than capital expenditures.

The trend is informative. From 2003 to 2008, 37% of cash from operations was used for corporate share buybacks and dividends (financial assets). During the same period, 47% was deployed for business capital expenditures and R&D (real assets). That was a full 10 percentage points of excess cash going to the direct benefit of real investment.

But the trend changed in the post-crisis years. From 2010 through 2012, overall cash usage moved in the direction of financial assets. Buybacks and shareholder dividends accounted for more than 40% of cash uses, while business capital expenditures and R&D accounted for about 44% of cash uses. So the 10 percentage point gap that favored real investment pre-crisis shrunk to a four percentage point gap.[3]

As the economic expansion matured — and monetary policy remained highly accommodative — a more significant shift away from investments in the real economy materialized. That is, financial assets gained a greater share of corporate wallets than business investment.

In fact, for years 2013 and 2014 combined, financial assets received 44% of operating cash flow, about one percentage point *more* than real assets. In 2014 alone, financial assets were the preferred investment by approximately 3 percentage points over real assets. That's a 13 percentage point difference from the pre-crisis period.[4]

For individual companies, the choice of "shareholder-friendly" distributions over investment in a new factory is difficult to second-guess. But public policy should not systematically favor investments in "paper assets" over investments in the real economy. Yet the conduct of economic policy — tax policy, regulatory policy, and monetary policy — during the post-crisis period may well have caused real assets to be a disfavored investment.

Monetary policy and the move toward financial assets
We focus on monetary policy because of its outsized role in the policy response in recent years. And we proffer a rationale for why financial assets might well be favored by the extraordinary conduct of monetary policy.

By the middle of 2008, the Federal Reserve observed falling financial asset prices in the United States. Weakening credit markets harmed bank balance sheets and undermined market confidence. Households and businesses pulled back on spending and investment. Actual economic performance fell dramatically, which, in turn, caused asset prices to fall further. A financial panic had taken hold.

The Fed responded foursquare to the panic. It chose to insert itself between the real economy and the financial markets. The Fed's balance sheet, institutional credibility, and forceful language were marshalled to break the vicious cycle. It established an alphabet-soup of new liquidity facilities, and undertook the most aggressive loosening of monetary policy in central bank history. Lo and behold, financial asset prices responded smartly. The S&P 500, for example, nearly tripled from its 2009 low.

The Fed's policy choices in the depths of the financial crisis were an understandable response to extraordinary conditions. But the global economy long ago recovered from crisis conditions. And the persistence of extraordinarily accommodative monetary policy — and its prevalence around the world — may help explain the ascent of financial assets against the backdrop of relative malaise in the real economy.

Monetary policy typically works through several so-called transmission channels to influence the economy: the credit or lending channel, to change the cost and availability of funding; the foreign exchange channel, to change the relative value of exports and direction of capital flows; the confidence channel, to bolster the "animal spirits" and the wealth effect channel, whereby rising asset prices lead to increased consumption and (indirectly) investment.

At the point of the zero-lower bound for interest rates (ZLB), policymakers adopted quantitative easing (QE), whereby they purchased a range of long-term financial assets in the open-market. In the case of the United States, purchases included approximately $3 trillion of long-term Treasury and mortgage-backed securities, and agency debt issued by Fannie Mae and Freddie Mac. In the case of Europe and Japan, QE involved purchases by the central bank of a broader range of securities, public and private.

While no final conclusions can be drawn as the QE experiment remains in force, we contend that QE is unlike the normal conduct of monetary policy. It appears to be qualitatively and quantitatively different. In our judgment, QE may well redirect flows from the real economy to financial assets differently than during the normal conduct of monetary policy.

Consider, for example, the decision of a CEO or board of a large, publicly-traded company during the last several years. Profit margins are high by historical standards. Cash is plentiful, both from operations and easy access to debt markets. The company must decide whether to invest in real assets or financial assets. That is, the company could invest in new property, plant and equipment to expand operations, or improve its capital stock to make its existing operations more efficient. Alternatively, the company could choose to buy back its own stock, or engage in some other form of financial engineering.

There is a common litany of explanations for the paucity of capital investment by the private sector during this economic recovery. Many commentators believe it stems from a shortfall of global demand: companies would build more capacity to match greater demand. We are less convinced by this familiar refrain. After all, capital investment is driven, in large part, by expectations of demand several years out, the time at which the new investment would be complete and product ready for delivery.

We believe the novel, long-term use of extraordinary monetary policy systematically biases decision-makers toward financial assets and away from real assets. Why?

First, financial assets can be short-lived. Share buybacks and dividend payouts can be curtailed at any time. Corporate decision makers cannot be certain about the consequences of QE's unwind on the real economy. The newfangled nature of QE likely causes more risk-aversion than normal rate changes in the conduct of monetary policy. Risk-aversion translates into a corporate preference for shorter-term commitments; hence, the preference for financial assets.

Second, financial assets are considerably more liquid than real assets. If a corporate decision-maker engages in a large share-buyback to increase his reported earnings per share, and economic prospects change markedly, he can rescind the outstanding buy-back authority; if necessary, he can even issue new shares to bolster his balance sheet. This liquidity is not a free option, of course, and some costs apply. But the financial crisis taught an important, over-riding lesson to investors of all sorts: illiquidity can be fatal. Financial assets have large liquidity benefits over real assets.

Third, QE, in effect if not by design, helps reduce volatility in the financial markets. By purchasing long-term securities, the Fed transfers significant duration from the private markets to the government's balance sheet. Measured volatility in financial market prices, as represented by such indices as the SPX Volatility Index (known as "VIX") and the short-term Treasury volatility index (known as "MOVE"), falls. Any resulting reductions in macroeconomic volatility — affecting real asset prices — are far more speculative. In fact, much like 2007, actual macroeconomic risk may be highest when market measures of volatility are lowest. Thus financial assets tend to outperform real assets because market volatility is lower than real economic volatility. Put more plainly, central banks have been quite successful in stoking risk-taking by investors in financial markets, but have found far less success in encouraging risk-taking in the real economy.

Fourth, QE's greatest effects may arise not from its actual operations but from its signaling effect. If one part of the government (the Federal Reserve) is buying debt issued by another part of government (Department of Treasury), one might conclude that overall economic conditions are unchanged. Or, as Bernanke himself explained, QE works in ways that are imperfectly understood, saying "it works in practice, just not in theory." Yet multiple event studies in the United States, Europe, and Japan demonstrate that financial assets move higher when QE programs are previewed and announced, and suffer when QE is thought to be ending.

Central bankers might not intend to be issuing a "put" or providing downside insurance to the securities markets, but that is a widely-held judgment of market participants after successive rounds of QE throughout the world. Market participants may not be expert on the transmission mechanisms of monetary policy, but they can deduce that the central bank is trying to support financial asset prices. The signal provided by central banks might be the essential design element.

No such protection is offered for real assets, never mind the real economy. So, for real assets in the real economy, the benefits are far less obvious, and the results far less impressive.

The relative dearth of business investment in the real economy is among the most anomalous aspects of the recovery. While private investment represents only about 17 percent of U.S. GDP, we believe that its effects are larger than that static scoring would suggest. Inadequate capital investment means that labor is also underutilized. The impact of modest capital investment is apparent in the weak productivity statistics. Productivity – key to raising wages and living standards — rose at a paltry 0.45 percent annual rate from 2011 through 2014, the second weakest four-year run in productivity since World War II. That goes a long way toward explaining the mediocre improvements in median wages during the recovery. And these trends, if not reversed, could also impair the long-term growth prospects of the U.S. economy.

Productivity, growth, and potential

The weakness of the U.S. economy is consistent with a pattern of unimpressive growth in advanced countries since the financial crisis. Relatively speaking, the U.S. performance ranks higher than the UK, which ranks higher than Japan and the Eurozone. But total U.S. growth since the start of 2008 has approximated 10%. Comparable figures for the UK, Japan, and the Eurozone are 3.5%, -1 percent and -3 percent, respectively.

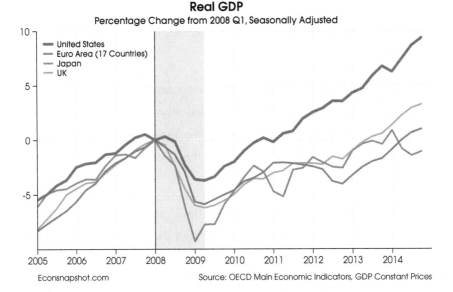

Real GDP
Percentage Change from 2008 Q1, Seasonally Adjusted

Econsnapshot.com   Source: OECD Main Economic Indicators, GDP Constant Prices

None of these economies are growing near their potential, as reflected in the cross-country data on economic growth, employment, labor force participation, or wage growth. In our judgment, they are experiencing a precipitous drop in their near-term growth potential, and the chronic weakness in the post-crisis years reflects structural and policy-induced impediments to growth.

Growth from the low point in 2009-2010 remains subdued. To fully understand the post-crisis growth environment, some background is useful. Coming into the crisis, leverage-induced credit and asset bubbles (not just in real estate) raised demand growth, specifically in domestic consumption, to unsustainably high levels.

How was such demand growth accommodated? Labor inputs (labor force participation and hours worked) expanded. And because the economies of the U.S., the UK, Japan, and the Eurozone are open, demand growth exceeded growth in output via an increase in the trade deficit (or reduction in the surplus).

The immediate post-crisis experience witnessed a reversal of these trends. Domestic demand dropped precipitously. Employment fell dramatically, and the trade deficit decreased. Initially, the drop in the trade deficit came from reduced imports (a natural side effect of reduced domestic consumption and investment), but then exports began to rise, and the supply side of the economy was moving toward external demand.

Errors in the conduct of public policy among most of the advanced economies have been a leading cause of the global slowdown. The excessive focus on monetary policy (as described above), the diminished focus on structural reforms, and shifts in the fiscal mix, slowed the speed of recovery and impaired longer-term growth.

Economists differ on the proper monetary/fiscal/structural policy mix. Some argue for a stronger fiscal stimulus to jumpstart the economy — though that does involve additional public-sector leverage. Others, including us, focus more on the conduct of monetary policy and the fiscal mix, the composition of domestic aggregate demand, and structural impediments to investment growth.

The level of public-sector investment is much debated. Such investment is complementary to private investment, and when it is too low, as has been the case since before the financial crisis, the returns to private real investment are also too low and private sector investment is suboptimal.

But, public-sector investment was inefficiently structured and misdirected, in spite of key deficits in infrastructure, research and development. Moreover, all parts of aggregate demand are not created equal. Poorly-designed public spending is a weak substitute for high returns on private investment in the real economy.

With the economy in its seventh year of economic expansion, some monetary policymakers continue to talk about normalizing policy. But given recent market turmoil, low readings globally of inflation, and downside risks to the global economy, it may well be that they have missed their window to act with any meaningful follow-through.

The remainder of the growth-oriented policy agenda remains ignored. And there are few signs that this will change in the short or medium run. One important step would be fundamental tax reform and simplification, with a view to eliminating special interest tax expenditures and increasing competitiveness. Absent tax and regulatory reforms, the medium-term outlook is suggestive of subdued growth, well below potential.

The subdued growth is not, however, entirely a function of public policy. There are also challenging secular structural shifts unfolding across the global economy, driven by technology and globalization, including China's growing economic influence.

The shifts can be understood by looking at the U.S. economy through the lens of its tradable and non-tradable parts. In the two decades prior to the 2008 crisis, the tradable part of the U.S. economy (about one-third of the total economy) grew, but there was almost no net job creation. The net employment gains (some 27 million jobs) were all generated on the non-tradable side (about two-thirds) of the U.S. economy. Employment and output grew, but value added per person employed did not substantially improve. Essentially, the middle income and middle range valued-added jobs declined in the manufacturing sector, while rising in the high end tradable service sectors like finance, consulting, technology development, and management of multinational enterprises.

Another significant shift in the U.S. economy involves information technology. It influences growth, employment, and incomes in multiple ways. IT has contributed to automation in both manufacturing and services. Routine jobs (defined as those that can be done by machines, computers, and networks) declined rapidly after 2000, and contributed to a further shift of lower and middle income workers into lower value-added non-routine jobs. IT-driven automation, coupled with the shift of jobs into the non-tradable sector, created downward pressure on middle incomes and contributed to a shift of the income distribution toward the top quartiles.

With the demand side of the labor market shifting rapidly in response to technological and global market forces, the labor market finds itself in a state of disequilibrium. In other words, the human capital, education, and skills base on the supply side have not caught up with the demand shifts. That catch-up process clearly takes time. A number of policies can accelerate the transition: placing more emphasis on core STEM disciplines in education, undoing ill-advised regulations, increasing growth-enabling immigration, liberalizing trade in high-technology goods, and increasing funding for research and development.

Structural shifts are clearly impacting the U.S. economy, but the advent of new technologies are making it difficult to measure the precise impact. Consider that an array of Internet-based services are free, while many other services are delivered at low and declining costs. While difficult to measure precisely, the pace of real value creation appears to be much faster than the pace of growth of market-based transactions in the information technology and services sectors. GDP data, which is calculated largely based on market transaction and prices, does not fully reflect adjustments for quality shifts. And as Harvard economist Martin Feldstein has pointed out, valuable free services are not counted at all.

There may also be delays between when technologies are adopted and when they are reflected in the economic data. Robert Solow and Stephen Roach separately argued in the 1980s that an extended period of investment in computers and information technology starting in the late 1960s appeared to have produced very little measurable effect on productivity. Then there was a productivity spurt in the 1990s that coincided with the wide availability of the Internet. James Manyika and Martin Baily, both of McKinsey, suggest that the current waves of powerful technology (advanced automation, artificial intelligence, 3D printing, and the internet of things) may have substantial long-run productivity effects, but with similar long lags. Both lines of argument strongly suggest that growth in real value created for businesses and consumers may be subject to under-estimation, in which case the productivity shortfall may be less severe than the GDP-based numbers alone suggest.

Nonetheless, in our judgment, attaining higher productivity rates is essential to improving long-term economic potential. And the dearth of real capital investment is making it harder for the unemployed and underemployed to re-enter the labor markets in force. Sub-par productivity gains are also causing median wage growth to stagnate.

The bottom line for advanced countries is that unbalanced policy mixes and structural impediments are contributing to suboptimal growth and downside economic risks. Longer-term trends are also creating structural transition challenges that must be addressed.

The challenges in China

The economic slowdown in China is as much a catalyst as a cause, of recent deterioration in the global economy. China's interconnectedness to the rest of the world manifests itself in trade, capital flows, asset prices and financial conditions.

China's economic slowdown reflects problems in the global economy. In most open economies, countries are vulnerable to significant, if not systemic, difficulties when weaknesses manifest themselves abroad. China is no exception. Specifically, the export sector has been an important engine of growth. The crisis of 2008 caused the Chinese export sector to lose momentum. Three percent cumulative global growth since the crisis in its major markets in advanced countries (accounting for half of global GDP) has caused the export driver for China to face significant headwinds.

The other main driver of growth in China has been public and private investment. It is running at a contribution rate of about 45 percent of GDP – an extraordinarily large number for any economy. And there is evidence that the Chinese economy has become over-reliant on investment to drive economic growth. This is especially problematic if capital is not allocated to its highest and best use. One such piece of evidence is a declining incremental capital output ratio. Excess investment with low returns at the margin will not sustainably drive growth in the future. The needed productivity growth will have to come from structural change, innovation, and total factor productivity growth.

Unlike many other countries, China's slowdown has not been driven entirely by suboptimal policy mixes and weak global economic conditions. It is also the inevitable result of a complex middle-income transition. Very few countries have sustained growth rates near 7 percent while making such a transition, and there are no countries that have done so while generating double-digit growth. Most middle-income transitions produce decelerations to low single digits (hence the widely-used term, "middle income trap"). No country has accomplished a middle-income transition at China's scale, and particularly not during a period of global economic underperformance. But, with improved conduct of economic policy, it remains possible to expect China to achieve growth above 6 percent over the medium-term.

On the demand side of the Chinese economy, a sustainable growth pattern requires a shift in the composition of demand to consumption and essential government services and away from investment. Consumption is just 36 percent of GDP (even after very large increases in wages in the recent period), though this may just be starting to change in favor of consumption. Based on international comparisons, a more normal rate of consumption would approximate 50-60 percent.

There are a number of reasons for the stubbornly low level of consumption. Chinese households are high savers, both by culture and necessity. The margin buying in the recent stock market bubbles is an abnormal exception. Equity in home purchases is normally in the range of 30-50 percent, and is mandated not to fall below 30 percent. The country's social security systems are also underdeveloped, producing high levels of precautionary saving, though this is beginning to change. But, perhaps most important, household income (which is largely labor income) is a relatively low fraction of GDP by international standards (under 60 percent at present) and, until recently, has trended downward.

The reasons for the low level of household income, as a share of national income, are not fully understood. But there are known contributing factors. The government sector owns a large share of capital stock and a large share of assets. The return on those assets, however low, flows to the government. Household savings options, until recently, have also been significantly limited by regulation, and deposit rates have been kept low by the government to fuel the investment-led growth model. Real estate has been the only other option for investment, creating a catalyst for a real estate bubble. The newer shadow banking system has created other options, but until properly regulated, it is a source of new risks. Chinese officials are grappling with a mispricing of risk because investors perceive an implicit government guarantee for a range of non-bank assets.

The central government seeks to address these issues through structural economic reforms, but if recent financial market unrest persists, implementation will likely take more time. And there appears to be some resistance from powerful interests. Market participants remain concerned whether the domestic economy is likely to respond with sufficient force as investment and external demand falters.

That presents policymakers with an unenviable choice. They can stimulate the economy in ways that are unsustainable, which may distort or short-circuit the structural transformation, and risk diminishing the government's reputation for skill and deftness. Alternatively, they can be more patient, let growth dip, and focus on the structural shifts and supportive reforms that will sustain growth and income in the medium and longer term.

On the supply side of the Chinese economy, demographics point to some slowing as the population ages. Productivity growth also remains a challenge, especially as employment shifts toward domestic services sectors. And ongoing employment gains may become more problematic if the domestic service sectors lag and/or if the labor saving dimensions of digitally capital intensive technologies exert a stronger influence on the delivery of goods and services. On the plus side, the Internet economy in China is highly innovative, as Jerry Yang writes in his chapter. It is influencing a wide range of sectors including retail, finance, and logistics.

The management mandate

The evolving economic environment we've described can be a challenge for companies, but also an opportunity for those with the ability – and agility – to adapt. While we cannot predict the precise economic contours, we should expect that the next several years will be marked by new challenges as countries search for new sources of growth. Business leaders must closely follow (and understand) the economic forces that are unfolding close to home, in their region, and throughout the world. While day-to-day knowledge is valuable, leaders should strive to achieve a plan to seize the opportunities – and avoid the pitfalls – that will define the years ahead.

Just as important is for managers to work to shape the future. They can do this by engaging with policymakers on those issues that they believe can create new economic opportunity and help unleash higher levels of growth. While every market will be different, a few baseline priorities are universal. One is keeping markets open for the free flow of goods, services, and ideas and deepening economic integration. This takes on particular urgency amid a stalemate in the global trade negotiations that began in 2001, as well as emerging efforts to stifle cross-border data flows. Another priority should be rebuilding trust among economic partners, since that trust is fundamental to the everyday commerce that drives the global economy.

As Chris Caine writes in his chapter, developing trust will foster understanding about long-term priorities, while also helping to open markets – and ensure that they remain open. Business leaders should also help policymakers understand how their investments can be a catalyst for growth. This is particularly important given that investment in the United States remains low and, as stated earlier, often misdirected.

Conclusion

The legacy of the 2008 financial crisis is often used to rationalize weak economic performance. In our view, the conduct of public policy and the reaction function of private sector firms is a more fertile area of policy discussion. The global economy remains at a crossroads. The challenges of the post-crisis period should be confronted with the same willingness to reconsider policy that marked the crisis period. And the public and private sectors should be devising new prescriptions for higher economic growth, domestically and internationally.

Managing the Opportunities and Challenges of Innovation

Samuel J. Palmisano

Throughout history, there has been tension between innovation and employment. Fire, the wheel, sea-worthy ships, the printing press, the steam engine, the telegraph, electricity, the automobile, the jet engine, television, the computer, the Internet, and smart phones, all illustrate the historical back and forth between innovation-induced job creation and destruction. I fully anticipate this will continue as long as human beings seek better lives and have freedom of expression.

Let's take an example I have been personally close to. I graduated from college, and started working at IBM, in 1973. That was also the year IBM introduced its version of what seemed like a revolutionary machine at the time: bank customers could obtain cash, and check their balance, without having any interaction with a bank employee. When a bank in Illinois began using the technology (which *Computerworld* described as a "customer transaction facility"), one of the employees explained its impact: "Customers don't have to spend time filling out withdrawal slips and stand in line for a teller."

It's commonly believed that ATMs reduced the need for bank tellers. After all, much of what they used to do, such as take deposits and dispense cash, is now handled by a machine. Except that the number of bank tellers has mostly *increased* over the years. From 1972 — the year before IBM introduced the "personal transaction facility" — until 1980, employment of bank tellers grew 84 percent.[1] The numbers have bounced around since then, with an increase of more than 150,000 from 1999-2007.[2] Some of that growth was lost in the years that followed (coinciding with the U.S. economic slowdown and a significant decline in the number of banks), but what's striking is how many tellers remain (more than 545,000, as of 2012),[3] despite the existence of more than 400,000 ATMs.[4] And even amid the technological progress that would seem to make bank tellers an endangered species, their employment outlook is projected to be stable through 2022, according to the U.S. Bureau of Labor Statistics.[5]

The ATM example illustrates a broader point: even when automation is seeming to displace human capital, while also delivering greater efficiencies and lower costs, the end result isn't necessarily lower employment. Indeed, automation can create new sources of demand and contribute to employment growth. This is what often gets overlooked in discussions about innovation and frequently the automation it produces – it changes the nature of things: new types of work and new types of business operating models are created. For example, ATMs reduced the cost of operating bank branches, so banks often responded by opening more branches. Additionally, the proliferation of the ATM had a "multiplier effect" as it led to an entirely new employment sector: self-service. And with this came not only the jobs that go with the people who design and repair ATMs, but also with the new self-service technologies and business models deploying them.

In this chapter, I explore a number of issues arising amid the technology-driven changes to the labor market, with a particular focus on key management priorities that can help companies navigate through this era of fast-paced, technology-induced change.

Is history repeating itself? Or is this time different?

Some will ask: If there has been this historic tension between innovation and employment then what is new? Isn't this the same old reality that mangers have faced over time? Others are viewing the pace and significance of these new technologies to be different.

Using the U.S. as an example, the ongoing evolution in the labor market can seem jarring, and there is no shortage of apocalyptic predictions about what lies ahead. Gartner, the technology research firm, has said that by 2025, one-third of all U.S. jobs will disappear because of automation. And two Oxford University economists who studied 700 different types of American jobs have projected that 47 percent of these jobs are at risk of disappearing over the next two decades because of computerization.[6] Sound different? Maybe faster?

Well, it's useful to remember that the U.S. economy (like many other high-income economies) has been through many job-changing evolutions over the past few centuries. The United States was once a primarily agricultural nation — farming accounted for 70 percent of the nation's employment in 1840. By 1900, the figure was 40 percent, and by 1950 it was 10 percent. Today, it's 1.5 percent. Farming's decline was a byproduct of increased productivity as well as the emergence of new technologies that fostered progress and created opportunities to earn higher wages. Initially, agriculture's decline translated to growth in the manufacturing sector. But the same forces that shrank the agriculture sector also shrank the U.S. manufacturing sector, which has contracted from 20 million jobs in 1979 to about 12 million today. As manufacturing's share of the economy declined, services grew — today accounting for about 80 percent of the U.S. workforce.[7]

There's little doubt that digitization and automation are triggering changes that are on par with those unleashed by agriculture and manufacturing. But will digitization and automation ultimately lead to job losses or job creation? Opinions are deeply split, as reflected in the findings of a Pew Research Center survey conducted in 2014. Nearly 1,900 technology experts were asked whether they expected these technologies will displace more jobs than they have created by 2025. While a majority of the respondents said more jobs will be created, it was a very slim majority (52 percent). The remaining 48 percent said the technologies will be a net destroyer of jobs.[8]

Underlying the fears of automation and digitization being a net destroyer of jobs is the belief that few — if any — industries will become *more* labor-intensive in the decades ahead. According to this view, technology will become even more refined and machines will become steadily more effective as they can harness growing amounts of data.

Touching on this point, consider the following comparison, from a 2015 article in *The Atlantic:* "In 1964, the nation's most valuable company, AT&T, was worth $267 billion in today's dollars and employed 758,611 people. Today's telecommunications giant, Google, is worth $370 billion but has only about 55,000 employees." The writer also noted that just five percent of the job creation from 1993-2013 was in the high-tech sector, while 90 percent of today's workers hold jobs that existed a century ago. "Our newest industries," he observed, "tend to be the most labor-efficient: they just don't require many people."[9] One obvious question therefore becomes what will be the impact of innovation on the 90 percent of workers holding the 100-year-old occupations?

As I will discuss, these forces of change have always been and always will be a challenge for managers. I feel strongly that a fundamental responsibility of business leaders is to prepare their workforce to move to the future, no matter how difficult and uncomfortable that may be. There are a number of ways to do this. First, they need to stay aware of emerging technologies that will impact their enterprises. Second, just as important, they need to have a view of their industry's future and a strategy for "reconceptualizing" the approach to doing the work they do. And, third, managers will need to reconceptualize the jobs and skills needed to do the new type of work. By taking these steps, their company can seize — if not create — the opportunities of the future and the new jobs that will go with them.

Why it matters

Innovations applied to business are designed to increase a firm's agility and productivity — remember the ATM story. Agility and productivity have always been important, but they are fundamental in today's globally integrated, demand-driven economy.

Increased productivity is an outgrowth of capital accumulation or greater efficiency of capital and labor, typically stemming from new products and new processes. And while that sounds like a snooze, productivity is fundamental to a nation's economic health. It is, says Ben Bernanke, the former Chairman of the Federal Reserve, "perhaps the single most important determinant of average living standards."

For much of the post-war period, U.S. productivity grew at a steady clip — averaging 2.3 percent gains from 1947 to 2004. But then it began declining — and from 2009 to 2014, the average annual gain was just 0.9 percent. The economic columnist Robert Samuelson points out the implications of annual productivity differences: "At 3 percent, incomes double in about 25 years; at 2 percent, about 35 years; at 1 percent, around 70 years."[10]

The apparent productivity slowdown raises a question as to whether new technologies are being captured by the data (an issue Michael Spence and Kevin Warsh explore in their chapter). But the real issue for managers is not the productivity level of a nation's economy — it's the productivity level of their company. Managers need to be able to answer questions such as: Are new technologies being deployed in ways that make our workers more productive? And is the company pursuing innovation that can advance productivity in measureable ways?

Keeping pace with higher productivity and greater agility

Regardless of whether the official data is reflecting the ways in which digital technologies, coupled with the automation of labor, have been reshaping the labor market, I am comfortable saying that today's managers are seeing and feeling a myriad of changes. Growing numbers of people in the United States are working as independent contractors or taking part-time positions in what's often called the "gig economy." One recent study concluded that between 2002 and 2014, the number of people in the gig economy increased between 8.8 percent and 14.4 percent — thus exceeding the 7.2 percent growth in overall employment. The study also found that the number of independent contractors increased by more than two million from 2010 to 2014, which represented close to 30 percent of the total employment growth during these years.[11] This trend would likely be more modest if it weren't for the ability of people to work differently, remotely, and yet be connected in real time.

While U.S. government statistics actually show a modest *decline* in self-employment since the start of the 21st century, economists Larry Katz of Harvard and Alan Krueger of Princeton have found discrepancies in these statistics. They point to increases in the share of the employed population filing the 1099 tax form used by the self-employed and in the share of the population filing Schedule C tax forms, which are used for homegrown businesses.[12] For societal and business leaders the more important question is: does this rise of "the gig economy and gig workers" represent an acceleration of agility at the worker and firm level?

To gain some insights into the gig economy, consider the profile of Uber drivers. A study conducted in December 2014, involving analysis by Princeton's Krueger, found that 66 percent of the 600+ U.S.-based Uber drivers surveyed held a full-time job separate from their work for Uber. There are many different reasons why these individuals would be driving for Uber while also holding other employment, but other parts of the survey reveal a strong desire for autonomy. Asked why they were working with Uber, 87 percent said they wanted "to be my own boss and set my own schedule." And when asked whether they would rather have a steady 9-to-5 job with some benefits and a set salary or a job where they would choose their own schedule and be their own boss," 73 percent chose the latter.[13]

Uber might be seen as the cutting edge of the gig economy, but as our Center for Global Enterprise research is revealing, "Uber-type" platform companies are emerging across more industries all around the world. Accordingly, I expect more people in the United States and elsewhere will begin to experiment with or even transition to more flexible work arrangements. While some are lamenting that fewer U.S. companies seem to be offering full-time employment, and the security it can bring, there can be other benefits from having people work in a more connected yet independent environment. It places people closer to market dynamics, as they are on the front lines of entrepreneurship. There are opportunities to increase individual earnings by taking on more projects. And, it can force them to be more adaptive and resourceful, and help ensure that their knowledge and skills don't grow stale.

Reflections on management

Time will tell whether the apocalyptic forecasts I mentioned at the start of this chapter are on target. While I am acutely aware that technology can have a disruptive impact on employment, I believe that over time it translates to more opportunity and higher living standards. My optimism is a byproduct of my reading of history and also based on what I observed during my 39 years at IBM. Over the company's 100-year history, a lot of our innovations translated to dislocations for some people whose companies didn't adapt to new technologies. But those same technologies were stimulating job creation for others, and helping to create entirely new sectors of the economy. For example, the rise of the electric typewriter accelerated "written word production," but word processors put the typewriter out of business — just as the PC put the word processor out of business. All of these innovations *changed* the nature of the work but the essential work of written communication remained.

However, we do need to acknowledge that new innovation-driven employment opportunities aren't necessarily distributed equally. They commonly go to those companies — and those individuals — who move quickly to adapt to the emerging technologies. But even that doesn't assure success. Managers also need to adapt to changes in the workplace. For example, it's already evident that many employees have different expectations from employers than in the past — in short, they want more flexibility — and in countries such as the United States, there's more job hopping than in the past. Managers need to be attuned to evolutions in employee expectations if they are going to retain their employees and keep them motivated to perform.

Managers will be confronted with a number of issues as industries and markets continue to evolve. As indicated previously, managers will need to be aware of emerging technologies and develop an understanding of how they can be harnessed to their company's advantage. Two key questions include: What new service proposition (or what new company) is enabled by a particular technology? And what are the implications for my company's business model? Countless established companies have never developed answers to these questions — leading them to long-term decline and, eventually, dissolution. Managers don't necessarily need to be technologists to succeed, as Jerry Yang writes in his chapter. But they need to have an awareness of emerging technologies and the threats they pose as well as the opportunities they present.

Consider the application of big data and diagnostics to the practice of medicine. It's going to mean that knowledge is much more widely dispersed. The all-knowing medical "gurus" who were once summoned for their expert opinion will be replaced by managers who can function as aggregators or assemblers of expert-level information.

Another priority for management must be to focus on preparing its workforce for the change. That means addressing the skill gaps created by the infusion of new technologies or the automation of existing work flows. Management needs to retrain people and modernize its workforce, helping to create opportunity for all. Equally important will be communications about just what "change" means. Management will need to articulate that there's likely to be an evolution in the kinds of jobs a company offers. This should be communicated in the context of where the strategy of the company is leading and why it's the right thing to do.

For this approach to succeed, the company culture must be one in which employees are adaptive and do not instinctively resist change. That's hard (as I learned at IBM). People develop an emotional attachment to the sources of their prior successes — especially when their businesses and *ways of doing business* are well established and very profitable. Proposing to overhaul these businesses — perhaps even sell them off — generates resistance, from colleagues, from shareholders, and from the chattering classes. But if companies want to differentiate themselves, they have to be willing to reinvent themselves. Developing that company culture can take years — and as Doug Haynes writes in his chapter, requires constant vigilance by management if a firm is to be successful.

Another area that is being reshaped by evolving employee expectations and needs is employee benefits. For millennials who have grown up in a more demand-side economy the employee benefit packages of their older siblings and parents don't seem as compelling as the food, transportation, fitness, and flex-time offerings frequently found connected to new "start-ups" and platform companies. Managers will need to rethink benefit packages offered to employees. If the goal is to attract and retain people who are innovative and entrepreneurial, and who don't want traditional terms and conditions, one way to achieve that is to offer innovative cafeteria-style benefits. Under such an arrangement, there would be an ecosystem of service providers for health care, retirement, and other benefits, and people would choose what benefits to receive based on their personal situation or their careers. Different employees have different needs, and the needs of each employee evolve over time. To that end, just as employees need to be adaptive with their skills, so to do employers need to offer benefits that are adaptable — they should try to optimize for flexibility and choice rather than one size fits all. This will help align benefits offerings with the ways in which people are increasingly living their lives and making choices.

The other reality companies must confront is that much of the world is in a slower growth environment than it was a decade ago. China, in particular, is growing at rates slower than at any point in the past two decades. Given these macro factors, *new* companies have the benefit of creating goods and services that are not tethered to the economic conditions of the past. But *existing* companies have the challenge of figuring out how to take their offerings and make them much more innovative and efficient based on new technologies.

My fellow *Growing Global* co-authors have shared their insights on six core management elements, which serve as the foundation for the Center for Global Enterprise's research and learning. Thinking about these six in the context of my topic, below are some of my initial instincts about the impact automation and innovation might have on them. All will require deeper analysis, and each is important for responsible managers to bear down on if they are to lead and set the pace for their enterprise's change, versus finding themselves reacting to the leading behavior of their competitors.

- *Supply Chain, Market Access, and Distribution Efficiency* —
  Thanks to leading-edge technology and innovative business models, which are illustrated by companies such as Chain IQ (a Zurich-based supply management and procurement company), firms can now redesign work processes to optimize local assembly, procurement, and scale. Additionally, as governments seek more investment to grow their local economies and jobs, market access will become a more delicate balance than in the past.

- *Economic and Financial Management* — In the past, centralized accounting and currency management were fundamental to the success of a global enterprise. Now with big data and more transparent markets, excellence in this area is not enough. Emerging classes of investors are more informed and engaged with the company's strategy and capital allocation plans. This activity will accelerate in a period of slower economic growth.

- *Building Government Trust for Market Access and Freedom of Operating Action* — An expansion of information transparency has made companies' behavior more visible to government and other external stakeholders. Using social media to finely tune your company's understanding of trending issues of interest to government will be necessary. And as governments exhibit more protectionist behavior, it's imperative for global companies to establish cohesive strategies and engage in dialogues that explain why they are valuable to local societies.

- *Creating, Managing and Protecting Intellectual Property* — Innovation is more the solution today than ever. Technology shifts like big data and cloud computing, as well as business process digitization, provide the solutions for growth and productivity. The IP assets companies create must be protected using leading-edge security technologies.

- *Company Culture, Leadership Identification, and Development* — Building a culture where employees engage the future and share in the visions of success is mandatory going forward. While this is easily said, it is very difficult to execute. Using social media tools to connect employees to the vision, and the needed behavior to realize that vision, will increase chances for success.

- *Global Versus Local Sales and Marketing* — Building a global brand is extremely powerful, but in doing so a company must not lose its connection with the priorities of the local markets. Big data and visualization tools can help companies calibrate societal expectations and determine whether the brand is fulfilling its intended value proposition.

Some things to focus on

Looking ahead, a key priority for managers will be monitoring developments in those sectors of the economy that are likely to have a transformative impact on their business model, their workers, and their workplace. Forward thinking can help mitigate the disruptive impact of these technologies and help pinpoint how to turn the disruption into opportunities for growth. As I think about the many sectors where innovation is flourishing, five stand out.

Robotics

Robotics have become a key component of production and they are an emblem of both the opportunities and challenges associated with bringing automation to workplaces. A 2013 McKinsey report pointed out that, "Advanced robotics promises a world with limited need for physical labor in which robot workers and robotic human augmentation could lead to massive increases in productivity and even extend human lives. Many goods and services could become cheaper and more abundant due to these advances." The report projected that by 2025, 15-25 percent of all industrial workers tasks in developed countries could be automated, as could 5-15 percent of manufacturing worker tasks.[14]

The growth in sales of industrial robotic devices reflects the deepening of automation in workplaces throughout the world. Approximately 225,000 robotic units were sold in 2014 — nearly doubling the number sold in 2005, according to the International Federation of Robotics.[15] These units serve a range of functions, and they are finding their way into more workplaces. As *The Wall Street Journal* has observed,

> Robots aren't just for the big guys anymore. A new breed of so-called collaborative machines—designed to work alongside people in close settings—is changing the way some of America's smaller manufacturers do their jobs. The machines, priced as low as $20,000, provide such companies . . . with new incentives to automate to increase overall productivity and lower labor

costs. . . . Robots have been on factory floors for decades. But they were mostly big machines that cost hundreds of thousands of dollars and had to be caged off to keep them from smashing into humans. Such machines could only do one thing over and over, albeit extremely fast and precisely. As a result, they were neither affordable nor practical for small businesses. Collaborative robots can be set to do one task one day—such as picking pieces off an assembly line and putting them in a box—and a different task the next.[16]

Robotics will continue to be fundamental to the automation revolution sweeping through the world's economies and workplaces, and they have the potential to make a big dent in the $6 trillion the world's manufacturers spend on labor each year. The biggest users of robotics, if measured by purchases in 2014, were China, South Korea, Japan, the United States, and Germany. They accounted for 75 percent of total sales.[17]

And it seems clear that robotics will continue to eliminate some jobs — and also create others. Robotic exoskeletons, for example, are like suits of armor that will give people — particularly the elderly and disabled — greater mobility and allow them to work in ways that wouldn't have been possible in the past. I expect that there will be countless other examples like this one — many of which we haven't even contemplated.

Intuitive computing

There is going to be a spread of intuitive computing, or what is sometimes called "deep learning." It involves the use of algorithms to "teach" software to be able to identify patterns — and reach conclusions — based on analysis of massive quantities of data. One emblem of this trend, and the one I'm most familiar with, is IBM's Watson. Because this technology becomes more accurate as it sifts through more data, it's been said that, "Watson is the only computer that's worth more used than new."[18] (While Watson is a computing system, and not an actual computer, the general idea is on target.)

The technology in IBM's Watson is now being used to help generate scientific questions that can help with the long-term development of new treatments for disease. Watson's cognitive capabilities recently enabled researchers at the Baylor College of Medicine to identify a key cancer-related protein over the course of just a few *weeks* — a line of inquiry that would have taken *years* had it been performed by human researchers.[19]

This is but one example of the way in which cognitive systems may transform how organizations think, act, and operate in the future. By learning through interactions, these systems hold the promise to advance knowledge of the trends underlying the complex systems by which our planet runs. Along the way, they will also be invaluable to new and emerging organizational forms that seek to create economic and societal value out of those systems.

Human detached mobility

Today, we think of Uber and other related companies disrupting the transportation industry and helping to create additional income for hundreds of thousands of people throughout the world. But amid all the hype about these companies, a longer-term view could lead one to believe that they may not have a bright future. Because if driverless cars become commonplace, demand for drivers will, by definition, dissipate.

There are many other sectors that could be upended by driverless cars. Assuming the cars work as planned, there would be a dramatic reduction in the number of accidents. That could lead to a severe contraction in the size of the auto insurance industry. Health care would also be impacted, given that there would be many fewer injuries and deaths from car accidents. (In the United States, there were close to 33,000 fatalities from car accidents in 2013.[20]) It's also likely that driverless cars would mean a decline in car ownership — thus impacting auto manufacturers and all of the related industries, including oil, auto parts, dealerships, and even car washes (which employ approximately 350,000 people in the United States).[21]

Drones could have a similar impact — disrupting the entire delivery industry (from the postal service to UPS and FedEx) while also reducing the need for cars. Routine tasks, such as shopping, are likely to become less common as drones are able to accelerate delivery times (they won't encounter traffic congestion) to virtually any location. But just as drones are destined to cause some employment sectors to shrink, others will likely grow. There will be demand for individuals who can design, operate, and maintain drones. There are already a number of American universities offering degrees focused on drones and unmanned aircraft.[22]

3-D printing

An intriguing technological development for all companies, but particularly companies operating globally, is the rise of advanced manufacturing, or what's become known as "3-D printing." A blend of industrial age and information age technologies, 3-D printing empowers individuals to create a range of on-demand products, layer by layer, based on computer models. This new way of making things will have profound implications for the manufacturing sector. Since mobile 3-D printing machines can be located virtually anywhere, and spare parts can be manufactured on demand (thus reducing or eliminating the need for stockpiling), the effect is potentially transformative: consolidation of supply chains, acceleration of production times, and significant reductions in fixed costs. McKinsey has estimated that the economic impact by 2025 could be $550 billion per year.[23]

Where 3-D printing gets even more interesting is the way in which it's likely to disrupt global supply chains. Low-cost manufacturing will henceforth be accessible to individuals throughout the world, as 3-D printers are destined to proliferate as they come down in price. That means 3-D printing may become a major challenge for developing countries, since their traditional cost advantage could disappear as manufacturing becomes more localized and less labor-dependent. And industries that have grown in concert with the expansion of the global economy, such as cargo (be it air, sea, or rail), could contract as products are created closer to end markets and end users.

While 3-D printing presents a challenge for established manufacturers, it is an enormous opportunity for small businesses, as decline in start-up and operating costs will greatly reduce the barriers to entry. And because virtually anyone can become a manufacturer, there could be a dramatic increase in new businesses tied to 3-D printing.

Asset models

In the industrial-age economy of yesteryear, companies' assets tended to be "heavy" — plants, equipment, vehicles, etc. In the information-age economy, assets tend to be "light" — software, cloud computing infrastructure, ideas, etc. Today, 70 percent of the market value of U.S. corporate assets are "light" (as Peter Evans writes in his chapter). These assets take the form of business processes and practices that flow from human capital (knowledge embodied in employees), values and norms (rules that enable the use of physical resources more efficiently), and tacit knowledge (unique business processes and practices).

The asset-light world calls for rethinking product delivery. The supply chain may not have a physical dimension; instead, it may be predominantly virtual. And the assets that were once found on a factory floor (which is physical) are more likely today to be found in the cloud (which is virtual).

That can facilitate a more global presence and lower expenses, given the reduced use of physical equipment and the need for fewer employees. In 2014, Facebook had revenues of close to $12.5 billion,[24] but fewer than 10,000 employees. While Facebook may be an outlier, it illuminates the value of "light" assets, and underscores the importance of management understanding how to reconceptualize their work and the performance of that work in order to achieve competitive advantage. Facebook unveiled a service in the summer of 2015 that would enable its users to transfer money. It may face obstacles in the United States, given that there are well-established payment systems, as well as some reluctance to link a debit card to one's Facebook account. But in developing countries, where the financial services infrastructure may not be as robust, and Facebook is a trusted entity, a money-sharing service could have broad appeal.

Conclusion

Companies and their managers face a plethora of issues in order to remain competitive amid ongoing shifts in the labor market. But the technologies that are transforming the labor market will place a heightened premium on skills that technology can't replace: judgment, insight, and leadership. While technology *will* be able to help managers sift through the information and the data that can guide their decision-making, the decisions about how to navigate through the issues I've highlighted will still need to be made by people. And as technology becomes more powerful, it's likely those people-based skills will take on greater importance. One research firm has found that some of the skills that will be in greatest demand over the next 5-10 years will include co-creativity, brainstorming, relationship building with customers, teaming, cultural sensitivity, and managing diverse employees.[25]

For those who continue to fret over the future of work, this outlook should be comforting. While knowledge and specialization are always going to be rewarded, so will other parts of an individual's profile. "The overall trend is a giant employment increase in industries based on personal interaction," writes Geoff Colvin in a recently-published book, *Humans are Underrated*. "It used to be that you had to be good at being machine-like. Now, increasingly, you have to be good at being a person. Great performance requires us to be intensely personal human beings."

For successful managers, the path to the future will be to visualize the nature of their organization's work in new ways and to help their future and current employees possess the skills required to perform within these new conditions. Those enterprises that have these two elements in their operational DNA will be on the side of change that is both creating the future and the jobs of the future.

Conclusion

Samuel J. Palmisano

About a century ago, the Ford Motor Company unveiled the Model T, which was the first car targeted squarely at America's emerging industrial-age middle class. Sales quickly skyrocketed and it marked the beginning of the automotive era. In the words of one writer, "The Model T put America on wheels, created mass mobility, revolutionized mass production, established the American middle class and eventually reshaped the country's physical landscape with suburban sprawl."[1] The Model T was the world's first mass-produced car, but it built on the engineering achievements that were pioneered in Germany. That's where the first car was patented, in 1886 by Karl Benz, and the first truly modern car (with a 35 horsepower engine) was produced by Mercedes in 1901.

Today, we are on the verge of breakthroughs that are akin to the original automotive revolution — what *Fortune* has described as "another Model T moment."[2] The next major evolution of the automobile — and its most transformative evolution since its invention — will be autonomous vehicles. Once they are commercialized, they are sure to disrupt the automobile industry, and many other industries as well. For example, think how driverless cars will give rise to new industries, as people devote less time to commuting and spend less money on fuel, insurance, upkeep, and even ownership. Might cars be more communal, and simply summoned when needed? Managers in the vehicle, and its dependent industries, are faced with a daunting task: getting ahead of the coming changes and seizing the opportunities they create.

The transportation revolution is emblematic of the changes that we see emerging across the business landscape over the next decade. Countless innovations will transform company operations and individual lives in the years ahead. New business models will emerge, as will a reconceptualization of traditional work patterns. These revolutions will unfold with great speed and scale, and their "tangible" character will evolve to a more hybrid state of balance with intangible assets.

These and other organizational trends reflect the future that's ahead for business leaders regardless of what industry they are in, what part of the world they are from, and what governance structure they preside over. In a recent survey of Fortune 500 companies, CEOs revealed their concern: 72 percent identified their company's greatest challenge as "the rapid pace of technological innovation." Add to this the heightened competition that results from a globally integrated economy and one can see a trove of opportunity and challenge ahead.

While CEO of IBM, I devoted considerable time and energy to preparing the company for the global era. I came away from that experience with a number of management insights, and the first edition of the *Re-Think* series, published in 2014, brought those insights together. They are reproduced here in abbreviated form (see Appendix for the complete text).

Management insights from *Re-Think: A Path to the Future*

---

12 Management Insights

- You need to be globally consistent but locally relevant.
- Learn to operate in many different kinds of environments.
- See your enterprise through a different lens.
- Encourage thinking and acting outside the company structure and outside the comfort zone.
- Know what you're good at—not just what you can do.
- Lower the center of gravity.
- Learn from below.
- Emphasize human capital. Employees have always been critical, but innovation-driven business models will cause skills to be equal to capital in value.
- See the world as it is—not the way you want it to be.
- Keep moving forward.
- Explain what you're doing—and why you're doing it.
- Create a common culture around common values.

(See Appendix for descriptions)

The foundation of those insights still holds true. In *Growing Global,* my co-authors and I have brought forth real-world business experiences, problems, and lessons in order to describe the new phase of globalization leaders are dealing with today and what they will deal with over the next 10 years. I have, accordingly, chosen to refresh the original *Re-Think* management prescriptions so as to align them with what we see as the current and future characteristics of the global economy. I offer the following eight principles to help manage the 21st century integrated enterprise.

- *You need to be globally consistent but locally relevant.*
  It used to be managers thought they had time to worry about this – and they did. But not anymore, since a company can have business around

the world on day one with a mere keystroke or swipe across a smartphone.

As both Shelly Lazarus and Chris Caine make very clear, companies operating in multiple countries need to tailor their offerings to local constituencies, all while ensuring that the brand's value proposition and the principles guiding the company are the same everywhere. In the age of transparency, inconsistencies are sure to be revealed – and can tarnish the brand in ways that are difficult to undo.

- *Learn to operate in many different kinds of environments.* In an era marked by rapid change, the ability to adapt to change is a key contributor to success. This is fundamental to my chapter on increased automation. Managers must be able to operate in different business models and employment conditions with one cohesive structure. They also must be prepared to seize those opportunities created by the same technology that is provoking the change.

- *Encourage thinking and acting outside the company structure and outside the comfort zone.* In an era of disruptive innovation that Jerry Yang describes, there should be a premium attached to disruptive thinkers. Indeed, conventional thinkers might well handicap management teams that, as Peter Evans points out, are going to need to rethink strategies, business models, leadership, core capabilities, value creation and capture systems, as well as organizational structures, if they are going to be agile and compete with emerging platform business models.

- *Recognize the value of intellectual property and other "intangibles."* Innovators will be the winners. David Kappos lays out well that as more countries focus on innovation, they are likely to become more aggressive in trying to protect their IP – and to prosecute those entities who they believe are violating national IP statutes. Getting caught up in IP disputes can be a major distraction – and a major expense.

- *Emphasize human capital and a common company culture.* A critical dimension of human capital is company culture, because as Doug Haynes writes, a company's culture is what defines it and holds it together – it's the connective tissue that will focus employees on the same set of values. A strong and consistent company culture enables exceptional performance, while a weak and inconsistent culture will often lead to disastrous performance. Just as a healthy culture can advance a company's human capital, an unhealthy culture can drive away the best employees. Hiring the best people, cultivating them, and retaining them will be a key driver of competitiveness in the 21st century, especially as organizational models become increasingly "light asset-based" and those assets predominantly are human. Thus management must tend to the company culture every day so it becomes part of the company's DNA and not a mere add-on.

- *See the world as it is – not the way you want it to be.* The global economy is projected to grow at a relatively slow pace through 2020. That's not an excuse for managers to reduce expectations. As Michael Spence and Kevin Warsh write, the slowdown underscores the imperative of developing a comprehensive understanding of economic trends – local, national, regional, and global – and engaging with policymakers to press for much-needed reforms as a catalyst for higher growth. Business leaders must be simultaneously agile and productive.

- *Explain what you're doing – and why you're doing it.* Companies and countries need to foster understanding about the measures they're enacting and how these measures will contribute to future competitiveness. As Chris Caine points out, companies need to be able to articulate their added value to government officials. What knowledge, service or product do you offer that distinguishes you from the competition and how does it benefit society and government? If policymakers can see how a company is contributing to progress in their communities, it will lay the groundwork for a sustainable and trusted working relationship.

- *Have a view about the future.* The innovation era that's upon us is likely to be transformative – for companies and for individuals. But fundamental to maximizing the opportunities of this era will be to have a view about the future and have the courage to go there. That's what Jean-Pascal Tricoire did – he transformed his company's supply chain and he placed increased emphasis on Asia, based on his belief that the world's economic center of gravity was shifting there. Going to the future – whether for companies or countries – inevitably involves change that's disruptive to (and resisted by) many. But standing still isn't an option. Embrace the change that's coming. Leaders must be all in and play to win.

As I noted in *Re-Think: A Path to the Future,* perhaps the most valuable lesson I learned from my 39 years at IBM was that the longer you wait to implement change, the harder it is to implement it – and the less effective it's likely to be. In a technologically-driven global era, the changes will come faster, they will come from countries – and especially cities – throughout the world, and they will be more transformative than in the past. Resisting the change is a recipe for stagnation.

Given the looming changes, leaders in business, government, academia, and elsewhere need to learn more about how to navigate the changes that lie ahead. That calls for educating themselves on the future, and the management skills required to advance not only their own success, but that of the communities they care about. The past is no longer a prologue to the future.

There are many ways to further that learning, and the Center for Global Enterprise (CGE) will continue its work to deepen understanding of how to seize the opportunities and develop the management expertise needed to meet the challenges of the technologically-driven global era. I hope you have found the observations and lessons in this book useful. *Growing Global* was another step by CGE to contribute to business learning and management best practices. My colleagues and I are excited about our work, as we believe the prospects for advancing social, economic, and human progress are greater than ever before.

Acknowledgements

Many people helped to make this book possible – not least those who agreed to contribute a chapter. Those nine individuals – Chris Caine, Peter Evans, Doug Haynes, Dave Kappos, Shelly Lazarus, Michael Spence, Jean-Pascal Tricoire, Kevin Warsh, and Jerry Yang – took time out of their busy schedules to share valuable lessons and insights, drawing on the knowledge they've accumulated throughout their distinguished careers. The Center for Global Enterprise (CGE), which is publishing this book and where I serve as Chairman, has been fortunate to have the active support of such an illustrious group and I'm grateful for their involvement.

I also want to thank everyone involved with the CGE for helping to turn the idea for this book into reality: David Beier, CGE Fellow, for his careful review and insights; Chris Caine, CGE President, led the project from beginning to end; Monica Consiglio, CGE Chief of Staff, for her keen eye and decisions regarding design, structure, clarity, and quality assurance; Kristen Palmisano, CGE Director of Media and Public Relations, drew on her years of experience in the publishing industry to help all of us stay true to our desired focus; and Ira Sager, CGE Vice President, brought his years of experience and skills as a journalist to help the text remain clear and as convincing as possible. I'd like to extend a special thanks to Matt Rees, who served as my co-writer for *Re-Think: A Path to the Future,* and once again was the literary genius and engine who got us to the finish line in an exemplary manner.

Endnotes

Did You See It?

1. http://edge.org/conversation/the-technium

2. *New York Times*, November 16, 2014. http://www.nytimes.com/2014/11/16/magazine/welcome-to-the-failure-age.html?_r=0

3. http://www.pewresearch.org/fact-tank/2014/02/13/emerging-nations-catching-up-to-u-s-on-technology-adoption-especially-mobile-and-social-media-use/

4. http://www.nytimes.com/imagepages/2008/02/10/opinion/10op.graphic.ready.html

Beyond Translation

1. New York Times, December 19, 2014. http://www.nytimes.com/2014/12/19/business/media/the-top-5-changes-on-madison-ave-over-the-last-25-years.html?ref=todayspaper

2. CMO Today, March 23, 2014. http://blogs.wsj.com/cmo/2014/03/23/cmos-work-lifespan-improves-still-half-that-of-ceos-study/

3. Wall Street Journal, September 25, 2014. http://www.wsj.com/articles/share-a-coke-credited-with-a-pop-in-sales-1411661519

4. Scott Bedbury, *A New Brand World: Eight Principles for Achieving Brand Leadership in the Twenty-First Century*, p. 110.

5. Jeff Immelt, LinkedIn post, September 5, 2014. https://www.linkedin.com/pulse/20140905115502-230929989-leaders-own-the-brand-and-the-ads

Company Culture: The Foundation for Lasting Performance

1. http://www.jimcollins.com/article_topics/articles/the-hp-way.html

2. http://www.hp.com/hpinfo/abouthp/histnfacts/publications/measure/pdf/1998_11-12.pdf#page=20

3. Point 72 Asset Management

4. Vega Factor's book, *Primed to Perform,* includes a chapter based on their work with Point 72 Asset Management.

5. https://www.linkedin.com/pulse/20140424002919-13378252-don-t-f-ck-up-the-culture

6. Arun Sundararajan, "What Airbnb Gets About Culture That Uber Doesn't," Harvard Business Review, November 27, 2014. https://hbr.org/2014/11/what-airbnb-gets-about-culture-that-uber-doesnt

A Market Force Like No Other

1. Dag Detter and Stefan Fölster, *The Public Wealth of Nations.*

2. https://www.wto.org/english/tratop_e/gproc_e/gproc_e.htm

3. http://siteresources.worldbank.org/INTTRADERESEARCH/Resources/544824-1272916036631/TTBDReport_June2014.pdf

4. These rankings are condensed from the World Economic Forum's more comprehensive measure of more than 100 economies throughout the world. The G-20 countries are ranked here based on the order in which each country appears in the rankings.

5. Only 19 countries are listed because one member of the G-20 is the European Union, which is not included in the WEF rankings.

6. http://www2.itif.org/2015-beyond-usa-freedom-act.pdf?_ga=1.5755827.1676278426.1433888498

A 20-Year Arc of Rapid Change and Innovative Disruption

1. Wired, February 12, 2015. http://www.wired.com/2015/02/may-never-use-xiao-mis-phones-theyll-change-life-anyway/

2. http://qz.com/294710/by-2018-china-will-spend-more-online-than-the-rest-of-the-world-combined/

3. The Economist, July 11, 2015. http://www.economist.com/news/busi-ness/21657376-sceptics-exaggerate-some-industries-chinese-firms-are-innova-tive-calibrating-chinese

4. Fast Company, May 13, 2015. http://www.fastcompany.com/3045708/big-ti-ny-problems-for-quantum-computing

Forces of Change: Networks, Data and Platforms

1. Peter C. Evans and Michael F. Farina, *The Age of Gas and the Power of Networks*, General Electric, 2013.

2. http://www.kpcb.com/internet-trends

3. http://www.kpcb.com/internet-trends (slide 45)

4. "IBM Unveils New Technology to Connect a Smarter Planet," IBM press release, April 29, 2013. http://www-03.ibm.com/press/us/en/pressrelease/40926.wss#_edn1

5. Wikibon, Big Data Market Forecast, 2013-2017.

6. Peter Evans, "Big Data for Economists: Promise and Perils," NABE Big Data at Work Conference, Federal Reserve Bank of Boston, June 14, 2015

7. Vyatkin, Valeriy. "Software engineering in industrial automation: State-of-the-art review." Industrial Informatics, IEEE Transactions on 9, no. 3, 2013, pp. 1234-1249.

8. Roberto Rigobon, "From Organic Data to Designed Data," NABE Big Data at Work Conference, Federal Reserve Bank of Boston, June 14, 2015.

9. Geoffrey G. Parker, Marshall W. Van Alstyne and Sangeet Paul Choudary, Plat-form Revolution: How Networked Markets Are Transforming the Economy, New York: W. W. Norton & Company, (forthcoming), 2016.

10. Brad Stone, *The Everything Store: Jeff Bezos and the Age of Amazon*, New York: Little, Brown and Co. 2011, p. 126.

11. https://www.youtube.com/yt/press/statistics.html

12. http://www.emc.com/collateral/analyst-reports/idc-the-digital-universe-in-2020.pdf

13. http://www.crn.com/slide-shows/data-center/300076709/2015-big-data-100-data-management.htm

14. Forbes, January 8, 2015. http://www.forbes.com/sites/ewanspence/2015/01/08/app-store-2014-10-billion-dollars/

15. Sangeet Paul Choudary, "India Platforms: Survey of Regional Dynamics," Platform Research Symposium, Questrom School of Business, Boston University, July 9, 2015.

16. Olayinka David-West, "Dynamics of African Platforms: A Survey of Digital Platforms in Sub-Saharan Africa," Center for Global Enterprise, June 2015.

17. Annabelle Gawer and Peter C. Evans, European Platforms, Platform Research Symposium, Questrom School of Business, Boston University, July 9, 2015.

18. European Commission, "A Digital Single Market for Europe: Commission Sets Out 16 Initiatives to Make it Happen," Brussels, May 6, 2015.

19. New York Times, June 11, 2014. http://www.nytimes.com/2014/06/12/technology/personaltech/with-ubers-cars-maybe-we-dont-need-our-own.html?_r=0

20. Dieter Zetsche, "Determination is Paying Off," Annual Shareholders' Meeting of Daimler AG, Berlin, April 9, 2014, p. 13.

21. http://media.daimler.com/dcmedia/0-921-656548-1-1511130-1-0-0-0-0-0-0-0-0-0-0-0-0-0.html

22. Baruch Lev, Suresh Radhakrishnan and Peter C. Evans, "Organizational Capital: A CEO's Guide to Measuring and Managing Enterprise Intangibles," Center for Global Enterprise, New York, NY.

23. Davide Nicolini, Maja Korica and Keith Ruddle, "Staying in the Know," *MIT Sloan Management Review*, vol. 56, no. 4, Summer 2015

24. "Shell Saves $5 Million with Consolidated Media Monitoring," Shell Oil case study, Moreover Technologies, February 24, 2009.

25. David Seuss, "Using Internet Sources for Market Intelligence," NABE Big Data at Work Conference, Federal Reserve Bank of Boston, June 14, 2015.

26. Edward R. Tufte, *The Visual Display of Quantitative Information*, Graphics Press, 1983.

27. See for example the elaborate visualization produced by Daniel McCallum in 1854 illustrating the operations of the Erie Railroad recently found in the U.S. Library of Congress. Caitlin Rosenthal, "Big data in the age of the telegraph," McKinsey Quarterly, March 2013. http://www.mckinsey.com/insights/organiza-tion/big_data_in_the_age_of_the_telegraph

28. WIPO IP Facts and Figures 2014, World Intellectual Property Organization, Economic and Statistics Series, 2015.

29. Hyoungshick Kim and JaeSeung Song. "Social network analysis of patent infringe-ment lawsuits." *Technological Forecasting and Social Change* 80, no. 5 (2013): 944-955.

30. Basole, Rahul C. "Visual business ecosystem intelligence: Lessons from the field." *IEEE computer graphics and applications* 5, 2014, pp. 26-34.

31. Martin J. Eppler and Ken W. Platts. "Visual strategizing: The systematic use of vi-sualization in the strategic-planning process." *Long Range Planning* 42, no. 1, 2009, pp. 42-74.

32. Trapti Sharma and Devesh Kumar, "Visualization Analytics for Big Data." *Data Mining and Knowledge Engineering* 7, no. 3, 2015, pp. 111-116.

33. Stuart K. Card, Jock D. Mackinlay, and Ben Shneiderman. *Readings in information visualization: using vision to think*. Morgan Kaufmann, 1999.

34. See R2 D3, A Visual Introduction to Machine Learning. http://www.r2d3.us/visual-intro-to-machine-learning-part-1/

35. *McKinsey Global Institute, "Disruptive technologies: Advances that will transform life, business, and the global economy," May 2013. Peter C. Evans and Marco Annunziata, Industrial Internet: Pushing the Boundaries of Minds and Machines, General Electric, November 2012. Published: November 2012*

36. Forbes, August 3, 2015. http://www.forbes.com/sites/parmyolson/2015/08/03/carmakers-nokia-here-google-uber-apple/

37. The Korea Herald, March 20, 2015. http://www.koreaherald.com/view.php?ud=20150320000722

38. Advertising Age, March 18, 2015. http://adage.com/article/global-news/ft-cnn-guardian-reuters-create-programmatic-alliance/297653/

Where Did the Growth Go?

1. "Real assets" — for purposes of this discussion — include real property, plants, equipment, and software. When combined with human capital, they produce tangible outputs that comprise substantial share of national output. "Financial assets," on the other hand, are but a rightful claim to the fruits of real assets.

2. Goldman Sachs Investment Research, August 2, 2015

3. Another anomaly is worthy of further examination: why the surge in M&A versus the muted capital expenditures? Why is the 'buy vs. build' decision for corporates not a fair fight this cycle? In our view, the answer may rest with the speed with which integration can be managed, costs removed, and pro forma profitability demonstrated. The conduct of economic policy in the cycle may well bias decision-makers to prefer share buybacks over M&A, and M&A over longer-lived business capital expenditures.

4. A review of capital expenditures alone (excluding R&D spend) tells a similar story. Cap ex accounted for only 27.5% of operating cash flow in 2013 and 2014. That's about 3.5% percentage points less than during the pre-crisis period. And share buybacks accounted for about 28% of cash usage in the last two full years, about 3.5 percentage points more than during the pre-crisis period.

Managing the Opportunities and Challenges of Innovation

1. "http://www.bls.gov/opub/mlr/1982/06/art4full.pdf

2. Wall Street Journal, November 17, 2014. http://www.wsj.com/articles/bank-tellers-battle-obsolescence-1416244137

3. http://www.bls.gov/ooh/office-and-administrative-support/tellers.htm

4. Finance and Development, March 2015. http://www.imf.org/external/pubs/ft/fandd/2015/03/bessen.htm

5. http://www.bls.gov/ooh/office-and-administrative-support/tellers.htm#tab-6

6. http://www.oxfordmartin.ox.ac.uk/downloads/academic/The_Future_of_Employment.pdf

7. http://www.bls.gov/emp/ep_table_201.htm

8. http://www.pewinternet.org/2014/08/06/future-of-jobs/

9. The Atlantic, July/August 2015. http://www.theatlantic.com/magazine/archive/2015/07/world-without-work/395294/

10. Washington Post, April 12, 2015. https://www.washingtonpost.com/opinions/middle-aged-capitalism/2015/04/12/31263982-dfdb-11e4-a500-1c5bb1d8f-f6a_story.html

11. http://americanactionforum.org/research/independent-contractors-and-the-emerging-gig-economy

12. http://fusion.net/story/173244/there-are-probably-way-more-people-in-the-gig-economy-than-we-realize/

13. https://s3.amazonaws.com/uber-static/comms/PDF/Uber_Driver-Partners_Hall_Kreuger_2015.pdf

14. http://www.mckinsey.com/insights/business_technology/disruptive_technologies

15. http://www.worldrobotics.org/uploads/tx_zeifr/Sales_go_through_the_roof_01.jpg

16. Wall Street Journal, September 17, 2014. http://www.wsj.com/articles/robots-work-their-way-into-small-factories-1410979100

17. http://www.worldrobotics.org/index.php?id=home&news_id=281

18. Geoff Colvin, *Humans Are Underrated*, p. 19.

19. https://www-03.ibm.com/press/us/en/pressrelease/44697.wss

20. http://www.iihs.org/iihs/topics/t/general-statistics/fatalityfacts/state-by-state-overview#Fatal-crash-totals

21. http://www.statisticbrain.com/car-wash-car-detail-industry-stats/

22. Washington Post, May 13, 2014. http://www.washingtonpost.com/news/innovations/wp/2014/05/13/graduates-with-drone-skills-are-going-to-be-in-demand-soon-heres-why/

23. http://www.mckinsey.com/insights/manufacturing/3-d_printing_takes_shape

24. http://investor.fb.com/releasedetail.cfm?ReleaseID=893395

25. https://www.oxfordeconomics.com/Media/Default/Thought%20Leadership/global-talent-2021.pdf

Conclusion

1. The Wall Street Journal, September 27, 2008. http://www.wsj.com/articles/SB122246777029780525

2. http://fortune.com/2014/10/08/drone-nation-air-droid/

Appendix

This is a reprint of the management insights contained in *Re-Think: A Path to the Future*.

- *You need to be globally consistent but locally relevant.* Companies operating in multiple countries need to tailor their offerings – be they products, services, or public policy positions – to local constituencies, all while ensuring that the brand's value proposition and the principles guiding the company are the same everywhere.

- *Learn to operate in many different kinds of environments.* In an era marked by rapid change, the ability to adapt to change is a key contributor to success. And the best teacher of adaptability is experience in new settings with new people. Once you decide to change you must communicate the strategy and get the buy-in of your workforce.

- *See your enterprise through a different lens.* You can gain priceless perspective on your company by finding a way to step outside it. Take an assignment outside headquarters – the farther away the better – and enmesh yourself with the local culture. You'll learn new things and you'll learn to think differently.

- *Encourage thinking and acting outside the company structure and outside the comfort zone.* All companies need disruptors – people who will dare to be different – and the most hidebound companies need disruptors most of all. Management needs to support and reward unorthodox thinking and employees need to develop the fact-based, pragmatic ideas that challenge conventional wisdom.

- *Know what you're good at – not just what you can do.* It's easy for enterprises and their employees to cling to a line of business because it has a history of throwing off steady profits. But the history of business is littered with stories of companies that clung to products or services too long and then found it was too late to pivot.

- *Lower the center of gravity.* Find ways to devolve decision-making away from headquarters and toward local markets. Execute closer to clients and restructure the financial incentives so that work with clients is more handsomely rewarded.

- *Learn from below.* Management misses out on valuable information by failing to tap into the knowledge that resides at all levels of the company. Leaders can't afford to be insulated by a protective inner circle that shields them from information they think will be unwelcome.

- *Emphasize human capital. Employees have always been critical, but innovation-driven business models will cause skills to be equal to capital in value.* The growth of companies – and countries – will be driven increasingly by brains over brawn. Hiring the best people, cultivating them, and retaining them will be a key driver of competitiveness in the 21st century.

- *See the world as it is – not the way you want it to be.* Recognizing how the world is changing will be a catalyst for game-changing transformations of how a company is structured and managed. But it depends on clear vision and strong leadership.

- *Keep moving forward.* Going to the future – whether for companies or countries – inevitably involves change that's disruptive to (and resisted by) many. But standing still isn't an option. Have a view about the future and have the courage to go there.

- *Explain what you're doing – and why you're doing it.* Because change is often disruptive, it can spark a backlash among those who feel threatened by it. Companies and countries need to foster understanding about the measures they're enacting and how these measures will contribute to future competitiveness.

- *Create a common culture around common values.* All companies – but particularly those with operations spread across the world – need connective tissue that will focus employees on the same set of values. And the values will be more meaningful if the entire workforce is consulted on what they should be.

About the Authors

Christopher G. Caine is the President and Co-Founder of the Center for Global Enterprise. He is also President & CEO of Mercator XXI, LLC, a professional services firm helping clients engage the global economy.

Prior to April 2009, Mr. Caine was employed by IBM Corporation for 25 years. For thirteen years he had corporate responsibility for global public policy issues that impacted IBM in his role as Vice President, Governmental Programs.

Mr. Caine also served as Director, Human Resources and Environmental Policy for IBM, responsible for public policy issues such as health-care reform, labor, personnel, health and safety, environment, and energy. Prior to that, he was Manager of Federal Government Relations and was Regional Manager of the company's state government relations programs.

Prior to IBM, Mr. Caine worked for the Coca-Cola Company, the Eaton Corporation, and the Electronic Industries Association.

Mr. Caine has spoken at a variety of public fora on policy and economic development trends involving government, innovation, globalization, global electronic commerce, privacy, and new security challenges. These fora include: United States Congress; National Intelligence Council Conference convened by the Center for Strategic and International Studies: An Open and Trusted Model in Information Technology; World Knowledge Forum in Seoul, Korea: Government in an Era of Rapid Innovation; the World Economic Forum: Improving Public-Private Cooperation to Address New Security Challenges; the Shanghai International Forum: Globalizing Electronic Commerce; the Progress & Freedom Foundation Aspen Summit; the Congressional Black Caucus Foundation; the New York Technology Forum: Transforming Government for the 21st Century; and the Centre for Corporate Public Affairs in Sydney, Australia.

Mr. Caine serves as a senior adviser for technology and public policy to the Center for Strategic and International Studies (CSIS). He is a Fellow of the International Academy of Management. He is on the boards of the following organizations: The Information Technology and Innovation Foundation, The Economic Club of Washington DC, The Institute for Education, The Ambassador Theater, and BrainFood.

He is a guest lecturer at Lafayette College and Georgetown University. In the spring of 2008, he created the Caine Scholar's Award for Global Leadership, Business and Policy at Lafayette College. It is designed to help develop the next generation of U.S. leaders for the globally integrated economy. He also served as an Alumni Associate member of the Lafayette College Board of Trustees.

Born in Rochester, New York, Mr. Caine received a bachelor's degree in Philosophy from Lafayette College in Easton, Pennsylvania and a master's degree in American Government from Georgetown University.

Peter C. Evans is a Vice President at the Center for Global Enterprise where he is responsible for the Center's research agenda and global partnerships. Previously, Dr. Evans held key strategy and market intelligence roles at General Electric. He was Director of GE Corporate's Global Strategy and Analytics team. He also led GE Energy's Global Strategy and Planning team for five years. Prior to joining GE, he was Director at Cambridge Energy Research Associates (CERA). He also worked as an independent consultant for a variety of corporate and government clients, including the US Trade Promotion Coordinating Committee, US Department of Energy, the Organization for Economic Cooperation and Development, and the World Bank.

Dr. Evans has extensive international energy experience, including two years as a Visiting Scholar at the Central Research Institute for the Electric Power Industry in Tokyo, Japan. His many articles and policy monographs include: The Age of Gas and the Power of Networks (General Electric, 2013), The Industrial Internet: Pushing the Boundaries of Minds and Machines (General Electric, 2012); Japan: Bracing for an Uncertain Energy Future (Brookings Institution, 2006), Liberalizing Global Trade in Energy Services (AEI Press, 2002) and Fettered Flight: Globalization and the Airline Industry with D. Yergin and R. H. Vietor (CERA, 2002).

He received his master degree and PhD degree from the Massachusetts Institute of Technology. He is a lifetime member of the Council on Foreign Relations and is a Board Member of the National Association for Business Economics.

Douglas D. Haynes is the President of Point72 Asset Management. Prior to joining Point72, Mr. Haynes was a Director at McKinsey & Company. Before joining McKinsey in 1992, Mr. Haynes worked for GE's advanced materials business, which is now part of Sabic International.

Mr. Haynes is an active community member, dedicating a significant portion of his efforts to supporting Veterans' initiatives. In addition to serving on the Board of the Robin Hood Foundation, Mr. Haynes helped launch its Veterans Advisory Board.

Mr. Haynes is also on the Board for Innovolt, a privately-held technology firm, as well as Singtel's Technology Advisory Board. He serves on the Corporate Advisory Board of the Darden Graduate School of Business, and the Board of the Canterbury School.

Mr. Haynes earned a B.S. summa cum laude in Mechanical Engineering from West Virginia University, and received his M.B.A. at the University of Virginia's Darden Graduate Business School, where he was a Shermet Scholar.

David J. Kappos is a Partner at the law firm of Cravath, Swaine & Moore. He is widely recognized as one of the world's foremost leaders in the field of intellectual property, including intellectual property management and strategy, the development of global intellectual property norms, laws and practices as well as commercialization and enforcement of innovation-based assets. Mr. Kappos supports the Firm's clients with a wide range of their most complex intellectual property issues.

From August 2009 to January 2013, Mr. Kappos served as Under Secretary of Commerce and Director of the United States Patent and Trademark Office (USPTO). In that role, he advised the President, Secretary of Commerce and the Administration on intellectual property policy matters. As Director of the USPTO, he led the Agency in dramatically reengineering its entire management and operational systems as well as its engagement with the global innovation community. He was instrumental in achieving the greatest legislative reform of the U.S. patent system in generations through passage and implementation of the Leahy-Smith America Invents Act, signed into law by the President in September 2011. Prior to leading the USPTO, Mr. Kappos held several executive posts in the legal department of IBM, the world's largest patent holder. From 2003 to 2009, he served as the company's Vice President and Assistant General Counsel for Intellectual Property. In that capacity, he managed global intellectual property activities for IBM, including all aspects of patent, trademark, copyright and trade secret protection. Mr. Kappos joined IBM as a development engineer. During his more than 25 years at IBM, he served in a variety of roles including litigation counsel and Asia Pacific IP counsel, based in Tokyo, Japan, where he led all aspects of intellectual property protection, including licensing, transactions support and mergers and acquisitions activity for the Asia/Pacific region.

Mr. Kappos has received numerous recognitions, including induction into the Intellectual Property Hall of Fame by Intellectual Asset Management Magazine, being named one of the 50 most influential people in intellectual property by Managing IP, and being named intellectual property professional of the year by the Intellectual Property Owners Association in 2011. He received a B.S. summa cum laude in Electrical and Computer Engineering from the University of California, Davis in 1983 and a J.D. from the University of California, Berkeley in 1990.

Shelly Lazarus has been working, as she would say it, "In the business I love," for more than four decades, almost all of that time at Ogilvy & Mather.

Shelly rose through the ranks of Ogilvy & Mather assuming positions of increasing responsibility in the management of the company, including president of O&M Direct North America, Ogilvy & Mather New York and Ogilvy & Mather North America. She was named worldwide CEO of Ogilvy & Mather in 1996 and Chairman in 1997. She became Chairman Emeritus in July 2012.

Shelly started at Ogilvy at a time when the agency's legendary founder David Ogilvy still walked the halls, and personally preached that the purpose of advertising was to build great brands. Under Shelly's leadership, that essential mission has remained the centerpiece of the company's philosophy, extending across regions and marketing disciplines, and attracting some of the world's largest and most respected brands including American Express, BP, Coca-Cola, IBM and Unilever among many others.

Shelly has been a frequent industry honoree. Advertising Women of New York selected Shelly as its Woman of the Year in 1994. She was honored by Women in Communications with their Matrix Award in 1995, was named Business Woman of the Year by the New York City Partnership in 1996, and Woman of the Year in 2002 by the Direct Marketing Association (DMA). She has appeared numerous times in Fortune magazine's annual ranking of America's 50 Most Powerful Women in Business. Shelly was the first woman to receive Columbia Business School's Distinguished Leader in Business Award as well as the Advertising Educational Foundation's (AEF) Lifetime Achievement

Award. She was inducted into the American Advertising Federation Hall of Fame in 2013 and is also a member of the DMA's Hall of Fame.

Shelly serves on the boards of several corporate, philanthropic and academic institutions: The Blackstone Group, FINRA, General Electric, Merck, New York Presbyterian Hospital, Committee Encouraging Corporate Philanthropy, World Wildlife Fund, Partnership for New York City, Lincoln Center, and the Board of Overseers of Columbia Business School, where she received her MBA in 1970. She served for five years as Chairman of the Board of Trustees of Smith College, her alma mater. She is a member of Advertising Women of New York, The Committee of 200, Council on Foreign Relations, The Business Council, and Women's Forum Inc. She has also served as Chairman of the American Association of Advertising Agencies.

Samuel J. Palmisano is the Co-Founder and Chairman of the Center for Global Enterprise. The CGE was established in 2013 to help educate societal stakeholders – as well as leaders from the private sector, public sector, and academia – on the globally integrated economy and its promise for a better future.

From January 1, 2003, through December 31, 2011, Samuel J. Palmisano was Chairman, President and Chief Executive Officer of IBM. He was chairman of the Board from January through September 2012 and served as a senior adviser to IBM until his retirement on December 1, 2012. Under his leadership, IBM achieved record financial performance, transformed itself into a globally integrated enterprise and introduced its Smarter Planet agenda.

Mr. Palmisano began his career with IBM in 1973 in Baltimore, Maryland. In a 39-year career with the company, he held leadership positions that included Senior Vice President and Group Executive of the Personal Systems Group, Senior Vice President and Group Executive of IBM Global Services, Senior Vice President and Group Executive of Enterprise Systems and President and Chief Operating Officer.

Mr. Palmisano is a graduate of The Johns Hopkins University. Among his many business accomplishments, Mr. Palmisano was awarded an Honorary Degree of Doctor of Humane Letters from Johns Hopkins University in 2012 and from Rensselaer Polytechnic Institute in 2005. In 2006, he was awarded an Honorary Fellowship from the London Business School. Mr. Palmisano has received a number of business awards, including the Atlantic Council's Distinguished Business Leadership Award in 2009 and the inaugural Deming Cup, presented in 2010 by the W. Edwards Deming Center for Quality, Productivity and Competitiveness at Columbia Business School. In 2013 Mr. Palmisano was awarded the French Legion of Honor for his many accomplishments during his successful career at IBM, as well as for his personal commitment to French-American friendship. He is also an elected member of the American Academy of Arts and Sciences and served as co-chair of the Council on Competitiveness's National Innovation Initiative.

Michael Spence is a Nobel Laureate for his work on growth in developing countries and on the convergence between advanced and developing economies. He is a Professor of Economics at the Stern School of Business at New York University, Professor Emeritus of Management in the Graduate School of Business at Stanford University, a Senior Fellow of the Hoover Institution and a Distinguished Visiting Fellow at the Council on Foreign Relations.

Professor Spence has also served as Dean of the Faculty of Arts and Sciences at Harvard and the Dean of the Stanford Business School. He serves on the board of a number of private and public companies and is a Senior Adviser to Jasper Ridge Partners. Professor Spence is a former Chairman of the Commission on Growth and Development. In 2001, he received the Nobel Prize in Economics for work that assessed how markets try to close informational gaps. He has published widely and is the author of several books and numerous articles and papers. His recent book, *The Next Convergence: The Future of Economic Growth in a Multispeed World,* describes how the global economy will develop over the next fifty years. It is available on Amazon.

He has a BA in Philosophy from Princeton University, a BA/MA in Mathematics from Oxford University and a PhD from Harvard University.

Jean-Pascal Tricoire joined Schneider Electric in 1986. He was appointed President and Chief Executive Officer in 2006 and named Chairman & CEO in April 2013.

His career at Schneider Electric has developed largely outside France in operational functions in Italy, China, South Africa and USA. Within the General Management, he served as Vice Executive President of the International Operating Division from 2002 before being appointed in 2004 Chief Operating Officer (COO).

Moreover, Jean-Pascal is President of the France-China Committee since 2009.

Jean-Pascal holds a degree in Electronic Engineering from Ecole supérieure d'Electronique de l'Ouest-ESEO ANGERS and a MBA from Emlyon Business School.

Kevin M. Warsh serves as Distinguished Visiting Fellow at Stanford University's Hoover Institution and as Lecturer at its Graduate School of Business.

In addition, he advises several companies, including serving on the board of directors of UPS.

Governor Warsh served as a member of the Board of Governors of the Federal Reserve System from 2006 until 2011. Warsh served as the Federal Reserve's representative to the Group of Twenty (G-20) and as the Board's emissary to the emerging and advanced economies in Asia. In addition, he was Administrative Governor, managing and overseeing the Board's operations, personnel, and financial performance.

Prior to his appointment to the Board, from 2002 until 2006, Warsh served as Special Assistant to the President for Economic Policy and Executive Secretary of the White House National Economic Council. Previously, Warsh was a member of the Mergers & Acquisitions department at Morgan Stanley & Co. in New York, serving as Vice President and Executive Director.

Warsh was born in upstate New York. He received his A.B. from Stanford University, and his J.D. from Harvard Law School.

Jerry Yang co-founded Yahoo! Inc. in 1995 and served on the Board of Directors and as a key member of the executive management team until January 2012. While at Yahoo he led a number of initiatives, including two of the biggest investments in the Internet: Yahoo Japan and Alibaba Group. He is widely recognized as a visionary and pioneer in the Internet technology sector, and was named one of the top 100 innovators in the world under the age of 35 by the MIT Technology Review in 1999.

Mr. Yang served as a director of Yahoo! Japan Corporation (TSE:4689) and Alibaba Group Holding Ltd. until January 2012; and a director of Cisco Systems, Inc. (NASDAQ:CSCO) from July 2000 to November 2012.

Yang currently works with and invests in technology entrepreneurs through AME Cloud Ventures, his innovation investment firm. Mr. Yang joined Workday's board of directors in 2013. He serves as a board observer for Lenovo, vice-chair of Stanford University's Board of Trustees, and director for Monterey Peninsula Foundation.

Yang and his wife, Akiko Yamazaki, are well known philanthropists who focus on higher education, conservation and the arts.

Yang holds B.S. and M.S. degrees in electrical engineering from Stanford University.

CPSIA information can be obtained
at www.ICGtesting.com
Printed in the USA
LVOW02*0437050116

469180LV00002B/7/P